Why the Cheetah Cheats

LEWIS SMITH

Why the Cheetah Cheats

And Other Mysteries of the Natural World

FIREFLY BOOKS

For Tolly, who missed the last one, and my parents, Pat and Harvey, with love

A FIREFLY BOOK

Published by Firefly Books Ltd. 2009

First printing

Publisher Cataloging-in-Publication Data (U.S.)

Smith, Lewis.
    Why the cheetah cheats : and other mysteries of the natural world / Lewis Smith.
[240] p. : col. photos. ; cm.
Includes index.
Summary: A look at the fascinating world of animals, their behavior, their use in animal research and the discovery of new species.
ISBN-13: 978-1-55407-534-8 (pbk.)
ISBN-10: 1-55407-534-3 (pbk.)
1. Animals -- Anecdotes. I. Title.
590 dc22 QL791.S658 2009

Library and Archives Canada Cataloguing in Publication
Smith, Lewis
    Why the cheetah cheats : and other mysteries of the natural world / Lewis Smith.
Includes index.
ISBN-13: 978-1-55407-534-8
ISBN-10: 1-55407-534-3
    1. Animals--Miscellanea. I. Title.
QL50.S63 2009   590   C2009-903279-1

Published in the United States by
Firefly Books (U.S.) Inc.
P.O. Box 1338, Ellicott Station
Buffalo, New York 14205

Published in Canada by
Firefly Books Ltd.
66 Leek Crescent
Richmond Hill, Ontario L4B 1H1

Published in Great Britain by
Papadakis Publisher
A member of New Architecture Group Ltd.
Kimber Studio, Winterbourne, Berkshire, RG20 8AN, U.K.
www.papadakis.net

Editorial and Design Director: Alexandra Papadakis
Editor: Sheila de Vallée
Editorial Assistant: Sarah Roberts
Research Assistant: Peter Liddle
Design Consultant: Aldo Sampieri

Printed and bound in China

Contents

Invasives

The Aliens Among Us

Invasive species are a common problem in this age of global transportation, when catching a plane from one side of the world to the other is almost as commonplace as going shopping. Wherever people have travelled they have tended to bring with them; sometimes deliberately, sometimes accidentally; animals and plants. Often these introduced species struggle to survive in an alien habitat, but others find themselves in an environment that is free of their natural predators, and therefore ideally suited to their rapid expansion. As invasive species spread they replace natives and their impact can change the entire landscape; especially on islands, where indigenous species are often particularly ill-equipped to fight off their challenge.

When the Cat's Away

A programme to eradicate cats from an island to protect native species has resulted in ecological carnage. Feral cats, introduced by humans, had already been blamed for the extinction of two species of bird on Macquarie Island and were taking a heavy toll of other seabirds when it was decided to exterminate them. However, an unintended consequence of the conservation programme was an explosion in the rabbit population which, without cats to keep their numbers down, caused devastation to the landscape.

Just six years after the last feral cat was shot on Macquarie Island, a world heritage site, the rabbit population had soared from fewer than 20,000 to an estimated 130,000. With so many hungry rabbits the 21-mile (34km) long island's vegetation suffered so badly that the landscape and ecological balance were changed. Researchers calculated that almost 40 per cent of the landscape had been altered by the rabbits, with close to 20 per cent of it suffering significant damage.

The Australian island, which is in the southern Pacific Ocean more than 800 miles (1,300km) south-east of Tasmania, has a long history of problems caused by invasive species. Cats, *Felis catus*, were introduced in the early nineteenth century and by the 1890s they had helped drive two birds, the Macquarie Island parakeet, *Cyanoramphus erythrotis*, and the Macquarie Island rail, *Gallirallus philippensis macquariensis*, into extinction. Rabbits, *Oryctolagus cuniculus*, were introduced in 1878 by sealers, and, despite quickly becoming the main prey of the cats, had sufficiently increased in number by the 1950s for their grazing to cause serious damage. In 1968 efforts began to control rabbit numbers by releasing the European rabbit flea, *Spilopsyllus cuniculi*, which transfers the Myxomatosis virus. The virus was introduced in 1978 and the rabbit population, which had peaked at 130,000, fell to fewer than 20,000 by the 1990s.

In the 1980s conservationists turned their attention to the cats, which, with fewer rabbits to eat, were taking a heavy toll of seabirds. An extermination programme was launched in 1985 and fifteen years later the last cat was killed. Within just a few years it became apparent that the project had backfired and that getting rid of one invasive species had simply enabled another to cause even more damage than ever before on the island. The damage to the environment worsened, because with the cats gone, the number of mice increased by an estimated 103,000 and the number of rats by 36,600.

opposite: **Rabbits are one of the invasive species destroying vegetation on the island** left: **Finch Creek on sub-Antarctic Macquarie Island before and after the damage caused by invasive species**

Complex mixes of vegetation; especially tussock grasses, bryophytes and megaherbs; have been replaced by short, grazed or bare areas. In many places rabbit grazing has accelerated the spread of another invasive species – annual meadow grass, *Poa annua*, from Europe. Observations showed that in 2001 the grass was present in four of eighteen locations monitored, but just six years later it had spread to another seven.

Satellite images recorded in December 2000 and March 2007 revealed huge changes in the plant cover on the island. The researchers calculated that when the last cat was killed, the rabbits increased their population by 4,000 in the first year, concluding "The unintended consequences have been dire,". More than half the females can be pregnant in a season and each doe can give birth to as many as 19 kittens. Even seabirds have been affected by the rabbits because their digging has destroyed the burrows of petrels, exposing the birds to attack by skuas.

By 2007 rabbit numbers were as high as they had ever been and the recovery of native vegetation witnessed during the 1980s and 1990s was wiped out. According to the research team, which included scientists from the Australian Antarctic Division, part of the Department of the Environment in Australia, the University of Tasmania in Australia, and Stellenbosch University in South Africa, "island-wide ecosystem" damage had been caused and further damage, including damage to the soil quality, can be expected. Macquarie Island was classed as a world heritage site in 1997 because it is the only place where rocks from the earth's mantle are actively exposed above sea level.

Evolution in Action

In little more than half a century a lizard under attack from an invasive and vicious ant has evolved new defensive mechanisms to protect itself. Eastern fence lizards, *Sceloporus undulatus*, can be killed by as few as a dozen red imported fire ants, *Solenopsis invicta*, in less than a minute, but have learnt how to shake off the unwanted attentions of the insects. Imported red fire ants have been named as one of the world's one hundred worst invasive species and in the United States they are costing the economy hundreds of billions of dollars annually. As the ants spread across the nation, they pose an increasingly serious threat to the lizards.

Fence lizards are only 3in (7.5cm) long and their usual defence when a predator approaches is to remain stock still to avoid being seen. A lizard will often stay motionless even when the ants have detected it and are trying to lift up a scale to inject its soft body with venom to paralyse it. But in areas where the ants have been established for several decades the lizards have both changed their defensive technique and grown longer legs to help them survive encounters with the ants.

Lizards in areas of the southern US where the ants had been established for almost seventy years have learnt to flick off the ants and flee. They had evolved longer hind legs, which were found, by Dr Tracy Langkilde of Pennsylvania State University in the US, to directly correlate to their chances of escaping ant attacks. As part of the study Dr Langkilde caught lizards in ant-free areas in Arkansas, as well as in two locations in Mississippi where they had been present for 23 and 54 years, and part of Alabama where they had been present for 68 years. At each site 20 males and 20 females were caught using a hand-held noose – a task made easier because the lizards remained motionless when approached. The lizards were exposed to ants on their colony mounds to see how their behaviour differed in each location. Dr Langkilde ensured that none of the lizards was injured, but they were exposed long enough for their reactions to be observed. A higher proportion of the lizards that simply

closed their eyes and remained motionless as the ants attacked came from the areas that the invasive insects had yet to reach. More than half of the lizards from the ant-free zone exhibited such behaviour. Most of the lizards from areas where they have experience of fire ants showed a far greater tendency to twitch their bodies to shake off the insects before fleeing. It was observed that body twitching was an effective method of getting rid of the ants and that the lizards with the longest hind legs were able to shake off the most. Lizards from Alabama, the first area the ants reached, had hind legs that were on average 3.4 per cent longer than those in ant-free areas of Arkansas.

Red imported fire ants are native to South America but reached the US in the 1930s and have become increasingly destructive as they spread. It is forecast that they will eventually colonise half the land on Earth and they have already reached the Caribbean, China, Taiwan and Australia. The ants are only a fraction of an inch long (2-6mm) but are aggressive, and by using their stings and attacking in huge numbers they are able to overwhelm animals many times bigger than themselves, even calves. The creatures they kill provide them with an important source of protein.

Studies of the genetic make-up of the ants have confirmed Mobile in Alabama as the place where the insects first reached the US, as accidental passengers on ships in the mid 1930s. Kenneth Ross of the University of Georgia in the US and DeWayne Shoemaker of the US Department of Agriculture concluded that the invasion began when nine to twenty unrelated pregnant queens reached Mobile and started colonies. At least one secondary invasion took place in another part of the southern US, and the total number of founder queens involved is thought to be just fifteen to thirty.

In further research, Dr Ross, Dr Shoemaker and other scientists pinpointed Formosa in Argentina as the most likely source of the ants. Identifying the origins of the invasive insects is an important factor in judging the likely success of biological means of controlling them. Red imported fire ants are genetically varied in South America and the creatures that kill them, such as parasitical phorid flies, tend to attack only those ants of a specific localised genetic make-up. If biological controls are employed they need to be carefully selected to make sure that the ants they are deployed against match those they would normally attack.

right: A lizard's scales provide no protection from fire ants
opposite left: A female fence lizard basking on a branch
opposite right: A fence lizard encountering fire ants on a mound

Mouse Massacre

A mouse has turned into a rapacious killer after being introduced to an island boasting one of the world's most important seabird breeding colonies. Birds on Gough Island in the South Atlantic were safe from land-based predators until the house mouse arrived, probably on whaling ships in the nineteenth century. The mouse, which usually lived on a diet of seeds and insects, discovered that the nesting birds provided an irresistible supply of nourishing eggs and helpless chicks.

The mouse turned to egg and meat-eating during the bird breeding season, and its numbers have soared to more than 700,000 on the 25sq.mile (65sq.km) island. So well has the mouse, *Mus musculus*, thrived that it is now three times as big as it was when it arrived on the island, but for the birds its presence has been a disaster. The mouse's predatory habits were discovered in 2001 and in 2008 it was declared out of control by the conservation organisation Birdlife International. One of the birds it threatens is the critically endangered Tristan albatross, *Diomedea dabbenena*, which breeds almost exclusively on Gough Island and is struggling to raise any young because of the onslaught by the mice.

Of 1,764 adult albatrosses which were observed incubating eggs in January 2008 only 246 offspring survived long enough to fly the nest – a rate five times lower that it would have been without the mice. The albatross chicks weigh up to 22lbs (10kg) against the mouse's 1.2oz (35g) but because they evolved on islands without

> The mouse flourished on an irresistible supply of eggs and helpless chicks

ground predators the birds have no defence against the rodents. The mice eat the chicks alive.

Gough buntings, finches that live nowhere else in the world, are just as badly affected by the predatory mice. In the last two decades the population has halved and it is estimated that there are fewer than 500 pairs left. Peter Ryan of the University of Cape Town has been studying the buntings, *Rowettia goughensis*, and warned that they and the Tristan albatross are "living on borrowed time" unless the mice can be eradicated.

Atlantic petrels, *Pterodroma incerta*, are one of five other birds threatened by the predatory mice and it is estimated that 500,000 of their chicks are eaten in their burrows each breeding season. It was recently estimated that there are 1.8 million pairs of Atlantic petrels, but they are in rapid decline because of the mice. It is thought that they will soon join the Gough bunting and the Tristan albatross on the critically endangered list. Less than 20 per cent of the petrels have managed to keep their chicks alive long enough to fledge in recent years and in 2007 the success rate was thought to have plunged to as low as 2 per cent.

Gough Island is part of the Tristan da Cunha archipelago, a dependency of St Helena, a UK Overseas Territory. It is a Unesco World Heritage site and, with 22 breeding species, is regarded as one of the world's most important seabird breeding colonies.

opposite top left: **A female Tristan albatross with a large chick**
opposite top right: *Mus musculus*, **the murderous house mouse**
below: **The Gough bunting is threatened due to mouse predation**

Tree Takeover

Invasive species of trees have been found to be muscling their way into rainforests where they can cause dramatic changes to the entire ecosystem. Arial surveys using a plane fitted with state of the art remote sensors have provided unprecedented three-dimensional maps showing where native plants have been replaced by introduced species.

The survey was carried out in Hawaii where the make-up of more than 850sq.miles of forest is being altered by invasive species. The study revealed that invaders are having a far greater impact on the eco-system than had been detected using traditional methods. Invasive species of trees were found to be taking over a significant and expanding area of the canopy and have such an impact on light levels that they change the make-up of the undergrowth. Such was the spread of invasive species revealed by the survey that researchers think it likely that the survival of native plants is under threat.

Two types of sensor fixed to the aeroplane were able to record the types of trees being observed, their height, the ground contours, the light levels in the forests and the quantity of undergrowth. Researchers could then build up a three-dimensional map of the rainforest identifying, with more than 93 per cent accuracy, where a variety of species could be found. Ten areas of rainforest, each of 121 to 240 acres (49 to 97 hectares) in size, were surveyed to assess the impact of invasive species.

opposite: **The slow-growing ohia tree is native to Hawaii**
below: **Invasive Canary Island fire trees dominate the landscape**

An estimated 120 types of plant are considered highly invasive in Hawaii but the project, led by Dr Gregory Asner of the Carnegie Institute in the US, concentrated on identifying the spread of five alien species at the expense of natives. Undisturbed rainforests in Hawaii are dominated by the slow-growing ohia tree, *Metrosideros polymorpha*, but it is losing ground to introduced species like the tropical ash, *Fraxinus uhdei*, and the Canary Island fire tree, *Morella faya*.

In some areas of the rainforest around the Mauna Kea volcano the tropical ash trees had grown to 108ft (33m) while at the Kilauea volcano there were fire trees 56ft (17m) tall. They blocked out so much light that most lower-growing plants died. The canopy formed by the invasive trees was 32 to 51 per cent larger in volume than the canopy formed by the ohia trees, which meant that only 2-4 per cent of light was getting through to the forest floor, compared to the 9-13 per cent allowed in by the native species.

Among the native species that were driven out of such areas were the ohia, tree ferns such as the Hawaiian tree fern, *Cibotium glaucum*, and ground ferns including the Old World forked fern, *Dicanopteris linearis*. In another area on the Kilauea volcano an invasive herb – ginger lily, *Hedychium gardnerianum* – had spread so effectively that it had replaced 66 per cent of the native low-growing species by forming a thick and impenetrable mat of root-growing stems.

Lowland areas of the volcano have been invaded by the fast-growing *Moluccan albizia*, *Falcataria moluccana*, which acts like a pathfinder for another alien: it fixes nitrogen in the soil which makes it possible for the strawberry guava, *Psidium cattleianum*, to spread and create a mid canopy layer of leaves and branches at a height of 32ft (10m), which cuts light levels on the forest floor by at least 95 per cent.

opposite: **Falcataria moluccana paves the way for other invasive species to grow**
below: **The invasive herb ginger lily has spread thickly across the landscape**

Stowaway Snake

A snake inadvertently introduced to a Pacific island is feared to be altering the entire forest ecosystem after wiping out the birds. It is thought that brown tree snakes arrived on Guam on a US military transport ship soon after the end of the Second World War and rapidly caused devastation among the bird population. The snake preyed unstoppably on the island's birds and it was regarded as a textbook example of what happens when a predator is introduced to an area where the wildlife is ill-equipped to cope with its assault.

Of the twelve species of native bird, ten have been driven into extinction on the island – some, like the Guam flycatcher and Guam rail survive in captivity – and fewer than 200 of each of the remaining two species survive on the island. Most of the damage to bird numbers by the venomous snake, *Boiga irregularis*, had been done by the early 1980s but the absence of the birds is now expected to have severe consequences for the forests. Already there are signs that without birds to provide free transport for their seeds the trees are struggling to ensure wide distribution throughout the forests.

Anecdotal evidence that Guam has substantially more spiders than nearby islands also suggests that the disappearance of the birds, which used to keep a check on arachnid numbers, has altered the balance of invertebrate life in the forests. Experiments carried out in Guam and on the nearby island of Saipan, which is free of the

above: **The brown tree snake**
opposite left: **Nets were placed around trees to catch seeds**
opposite right: **The Guam rail survives only in captivity**

brown tree snakes, suggest that over time the spread of trees will be completely changed.

Biologists from the University of Washington in the US placed nets beneath and around false elder trees up to a distance of 65ft (20m) away to catch all the seeds that fell. On Guam it was found that seeds fell only into the traps directly underneath the canopy whereas on Saipan they were caught at whatever distance from the trees the nets were set up. Researchers also observed that the outer layers of the seeds which dropped furthest from the trees on Saipan had all been removed. It is thought that they were stripped away while in the digestive systems of birds and that this treatment speeded up germination.

In a second series of tests the researchers inspected a number of randomly chosen sites on the islands of Guam, Saipan, Tinian and Rota. They sought out seedlings of a tree, *Aglaia mariannensis*, and the closest mature tree that was likely to be the parent. On Guam all the parent trees were within 16ft (5m) of all their seedlings, whereas on the other islands the distance was two to three times greater.

Haldre Rogers, who presented the findings to the Ecological Society of America, explained that the change in seed distribution caused by the snake could transform the forest from a diverse mix of trees to a series of single-species clumps surrounded by open spaces. Such a change would be catastrophic for large numbers of plant and animal species, with the likelihood that many of them would follow the birds into extinction. Some trees rely on birds more than others for a wide distribution, but all are thought to be affected by the changes because fungi that feed on and kill seeds are often found in high densities close to the parent plants.

Guam is now one of the most snake-infested islands in the world, as the brown tree snakes, some of which are 10ft (3m) long, are estimated to number more than 3,000 per sq.mile. With the birds now virtually all gone they eat mostly lizards and rodents. The only native snake on Guam is the tiny, blind species *Ramphotyphlops braminus*, which hunts bugs.

> Brown tree snakes arrived on Guam on a US military transport ship

Pirate Rats

Rats which infested the holds of pirate ships have been identified as the chief culprits behind the destruction of one of Darwin's finches. Mangrove finches are one of 13 species of finch on the Galápagos Islands, but they have been driven near to extinction. Fewer than a hundred of the finches were left on Isabela Island – their home territory in the Galápagos – when conservationists managed to identify the cause of their catastrophic fall in numbers. An emergency programme was launched to clear as many rats as possible from the birds' last breeding sites to stop them eating the eggs and the chicks. Controlling the rodents was successful in stemming the decline of the birds, and in 2008 more chicks survived to fly the nest than for many years. Moreover, enough chicks survived into adulthood in 2009 to enable the species to start re-colonising areas of Isabela that it had deserted when numbers crashed.

Black rats are thought to have arrived on Isabela, the largest of the Galápagos Islands, on pirate ships perhaps as early as the sixteenth century. Pirates used the islands to hide before sailing off to Spanish shipping lanes in search of treasure ships. The rodents were identified as the biggest threat to the finches, which inhabit mangroves, when Dr Birgit Fessl of the Charles Darwin Foundation was posted to Isabela to study the decline of the birds as part of a project led by the Durrell Wildlife Conservation Trust in Jersey. She saw rats climbing up to the nests to

eat the eggs and chicks during the finch's breeding season in such numbers that few of the adult birds managed to raise any young.

Two other invasive species were also found to be taking a toll on the finches. Feral cats ate a handful of the birds and a parasitic bot fly, *Philornis downsi*, which originated in Trinidad, accounted for even more deaths, but by far the biggest killers were the rats. According to Dr Glyn Young of Durrell, the problem was so acute and so few finches were left that a programme to reduce rat numbers by leaving them poisoned bait was launched immediately. The finches, *Camarhynchus heliobates*, are thought to have been found in dozens of mangroves around the island in the past but they are now confined almost exclusively to a small section of the north-west coast. They were were also present on Fernandina Island but died out.

Finches from the Galápagos Islands played an important role in encouraging Charles Darwin to develop his theory of evolution. He visited the Galápagos in 1835 during his five-year voyage on HMS Beagle and shot and took home nine species of finch. Although they were all quite similar, each had distinct differences, especially in the beak shape and size. Because of his work on the birds and their close relationship to each other they became known collectively as Darwin's finches, but the mangrove finch was one of those that he failed to bring home. There are 14 species

opposite: **Black rat**
above: **Mangrove finch**
overleaf left:
Warbler finch
overleaf right:
Woodpecker finch

of finch in total, 13 of which are found only on the Galápagos Islands while the fourteenth is found on the Cocos Islands. Darwin's finches, which are believed to have a common ancestor, are thought to have developed slight differences as they adapted to different ecological niches.

Floreana mockingbirds, the first species to prompt Darwin to start thinking about evolution, have been just as badly hit by invasive species as the mangrove finch. Darwin was quickly struck by the slight differences between the mockingbirds he came across on Floreana and on San Cristobal, fifty miles away. He soon noticed further differences in birds from other islands, but within fifty years of the *Beagle* anchoring in the Galápagos the mockingbird found on Floreana had been wiped out on the island. Floreana mockingbirds, *Mimus trifasciatus*, now only survive on two tiny islets, Gardner-by-Floreana and Champion, which are in sight of Floreana and provided a refuge from the hordes of invasive species that took over the mockingbirds' home. Rats were the biggest killers, eating the eggs and chicks, but goats caused just as much devastation

because they destroyed the prickly pear cactus that the birds depended on. Other animals introduced from Europe, such as donkeys, pigs and cats, wreaked yet more damage.

Only about 500 of the birds are estimated to survive but preparatory work is now being undertaken as a joint project between the Galápagos National Park, the Charles Darwin Foundation, Zurich University in Switzerland, the University of Missouri in the US, and Durrell to reintroduce the mockingbird to Floreana. Birds on the islets will be studied to ascertain their needs so that the chosen release sites will offer the mockingbirds the best chance of thriving. Before any birds can be set free on the island the release sites will have to be swept clear of rats and other invasive creatures, such as cats, which might threaten them. Similarly, the island suffers from invasive plants which will also have to be cleared from the areas where the mockingbirds are to be reintroduced. They will be replaced by a replanting programme that will re-establish the prickly pear cactus and other vegetation needed by the birds.

Cabbage Rescue

A cabbage found only on a small island has been given fresh hope of survival by a project to eradicate rhododendrons. The invasive rhododendrons out-compete the cabbage and were threatening to drive it into extinction.

Lundy cabbages, *Coincya wrightii*, are found on Lundy Island off the north coast of Devon in south-west Britain, where they grow primarily on cliff-faces. Since the introduction of rhododendrons in the nineteenth century they have been in danger of being overwhelmed. Rhododendrons thrived on the island and spread rapidly including into the cabbages' cliff stronghold. Attempts to control the invaders have been made since the 1940s, but each time they were hacked down they grew back even stronger.

From 2002 conservationists made a concerted and organised effort to clear the rhododendrons and they have been pushed back to a fraction of their former coverage. They expect that within a few more years the alien will be gone from the island. With the retreat of the invasive species, the native plant, which is edible but tastes revolting, has spread back into those areas cleared of rhododendrons, where it has not grown for decades. It has been able to spread more extensively in part because another invasive species – rabbits – has been at a temporary low ebb.

Rabbits were brought to Lundy by King Henry III, who designated the island a royal warren. In boom years the animal is considered a pest, but outbreaks of disease bring it back to less damaging levels and the cabbage recovers. Even when rabbit numbers are out of control the Lundy cabbage is safe on the cliff faces.

By protecting the cabbages from the advance of rhododendrons the conservationists have offered a future to the Lundy cabbage flea beetle, *Psylliodes luridipennis*. Like its host plant, it is found only on Lundy. Similarly, the future of the Lundy cabbage weevil, *Ceutorhynchus contractus pallipes*, is more secure.

Lundy cabbages, which have bright yellow flowers and can grow up to 5ft (1.5m) tall, evolved from a cabbage which colonised sand dunes at the end of the last Ice Age in what is now the Bristol Channel. After the ice retreated, the sea level rose and cut off the plant from the mainland, and it was able to evolve in isolation.

opposite: **Lundy cabbages growing across the cliff-face**
below left: **The plant's bright yellow flowers**
below right: **Lundy cabbage weevil**

Return of the Native

An invasive tree is helping to protect garden birds from some of the impact of a changing climate by providing them with a timely feast. Warmer temperatures have meant that in many parts of the world spring arrives several days or even weeks earlier than it did half a century ago. Earlier egg-laying is one of the consequences, but for many species of bird the change can be damaging because the chicks are born before their main food sources are available.

The introduction and spread of the Turkey oak in Britain is, however, providing a lifeline to several garden birds, notably tits, because it attracts gall wasps. Early in the spring the gall wasps lay eggs on the buds and these provide an important source of food for the tits' chicks before their traditional fare of caterpillars has

emerged. Chemicals on the eggs trick the tree, *Quercus cerris*, into forming a gall – a hard shell the size of a sesame seed – around them, but despite this protection they are easily picked off by tits and other birds.

Turkey oaks are found naturally in southern Europe and were introduced to northern Europe in the eighteenth century. They were brought to Britain in 1735 as an alternative to native English oaks, *Quercus Robur*, for the construction of ships for the Royal Navy. Timber from the Turkey oak proved inferior to the English oak for shipbuilding, but the tree became popular for gardens and quickly became established and spread. It is now found as far north as Scotland.

Researchers studying fossilised galls found that the Turkey oak was present in northern Europe until 120,000 years ago when it was driven out by the onset of an Ice Age. Once the ice retreated the trees were unable to return naturally because they had been pushed so far south that they were separated from northern Europe by the Alps. Researchers from Britain and the Netherlands concluded that having the tree return as an invasive species most likely re-established what was once an ancient and natural ecological balance in which tits fed on the gall wasp eggs.

The importance of the gall wasp eggs to tits struggling to cope with climate change was shown in a study carried out by scientists from the University of Edinburgh and the Centre for Ecology and Hydrology in the UK. The fossilised galls were studied by a team from the Netherlands, including researchers from Leiden

opposite:
Oak wasp galls
right: A gall wasp
of species *Andricus
kollari* emerging
from a gall.

Researchers concluded that having the tree return most likely re-established what was once an ancient and natural ecological balance

University, and Britain. Dr Graham Stone, of the University of Edinburgh, took part in both studies and was convinced that Turkey oaks complemented the native oaks rather than disrupting the natural balance of woodland, as other researchers feared.

Fossilised oak galls dated to 115,000-130,000 years ago were discovered in a gravel pit near Raalte in the Netherlands. The sediment they were in was deposited by the River Rhine, but they were dug up from a valley that now has the River Ijssel running through it. The galls were so well preserved that the fossil remains could be seen in three dimensions, which allowed researchers to identify the species of insect that caused the galls and the plant that was attacked for the first time. Two different types of gall were identified, both caused by oak gall wasps. One was attributed to *Andricus hungaricus* and the other is thought to have been formed as the result of an attack by *Andricus quercusradicis*. Both species are closely associated with Turkey oaks today. Galls 305 million years old have previously been discovered in three dimensions but it has proved impossible to identify either the plant species or the insect that caused them.

Ancients
Vanished Lives

Big or small, docile or fierce, long extinct animals that once walked the earth or swam in the rivers and oceans continue to attract our attention. Life on earth spans several hundred million years and during that time there have been endless varieties of animals to take advantage of any ecological niche. Creatures in the fossil record can appear in forms that are instantly recognisable, whereas others look alien because there is nothing comparable in the modern world. Uncovering the fossil bones, skin, feathers, scales, footprints or any other traces that have been left to us is just the start of our understanding the mysteries of life long gone. Where once scientists were content to work out how bones fitted together, these days researchers are able to interpret them to provide a much wider picture of the ancient animal's behaviour and the environment it lived in.

Sociable Sabre-tooth

Analysis of tar pit victims suggests that sabre-tooth cats, while far from cuddly, were sociable creatures that hunted in packs. Fossil bones recovered from ancient tar pits have revealed that the sabre-tooth, *Smilodon fatalis*, was trapped more often than would have been expected for a solitary animal. Researchers have concluded that they must have been pack animals who lived and hunted together like today's lions.

A third of the carnivorous animals preserved in the Rancho La Brea tar seeps in California (which date from 9,000 to 44,000 years ago) were sabre-tooth cats and just over half were dire wolves. They were probably lured into the tar by the panicked cries of prey species already trapped there. Cats and wolves would have regarded the helpless animals as an easy meal, until they themselves became fatally stuck.

Dire wolves are thought to have been pack animals, like modern wolves, whereas other meat-eating victims, such as the short-faced bear, puma and jaguars, were solitary creatures and became trapped far less often. The most frequently caught carnivore after the sabre-tooth cats were coyotes, which made up 7.7 per cent of all the creatures found, and American lions, which accounted for only 2.6 per cent. In all, seventeen species of carnivore were identified, five of which are now extinct. Nine times more carnivores than herbivores were found, supporting the theory that they were lured in by the cries of trapped animals.

According to researchers, if the sabre-tooth cat, which had canine teeth up to 7in (18cm) long, had been a solitary hunter, its population in the surrounding landscape would have been too low for so many to have got stuck in the tar. Furthermore, pack hunters would have had the confidence to approach an animal making enough noise to be heard over a wide area whereas solitary predators would have been more circumspect. In the wild today lone hunters are often mobbed by pack predators.

To test the idea that the sabre-tooths were sociable animals, researchers carried out an experiment in Africa in which the distress calls of prey species were broadcast from speakers. Recordings were played for 30 to 120 minutes at night, dawn and dusk to see how many animals would approach. Large social carnivores made up 85 per cent of all the animals lured in – a rate 60 times higher than expected on the basis of their numbers. The proportion responding to the distress call recordings was virtually the same as the 88 per cent drawn to the ancient tar pits, when counting the sabre-tooth as a pack animal.

Dr Chris Carbone of the Zoological Society of London in the UK took part in the study and said that the findings strongly suggested that *Smilodon fatalis* was more likely to roam "in formidable gangs" than as a lone hunter. The high proportion of juvenile sabre-tooth cats found in the pit also suggested that they accompanied adults just as African lion cubs do today.

opposite: **Artist's impression of sabre-tooth cats in their natural environment**
right: **Sabre-tooth cats attack their prey**

The Invention of Sex

The fossilised creature,
Funisia dorothea

It is unlikely that it made the earth move, but the first time sex was enjoyed, or at least performed, by an animal has been dated to 570 million years ago. A mysterious fossilised organism has been identified as the first animal to have had sex and its discovery has provided fresh insights into the complexity of the earliest ecosystems.

Funisia dorothea was a knobbly, rope-like creature which grew to about 12in (30cm) long and lived on sandy areas of the sea floor during the Neoproterozoic era, which lasted about 100 million years and ended 540 million years ago. Little is known of the creature, which was dug up in Australia, but it is thought that it reproduced sexually during simultaneous spawn-

Funisia dorothea was a knobbly, rope-like creature

ings of many individuals, much as modern corals and sponges do.

Researchers concluded the creature reproduced sexually, rather than asexually, because the individuals found in groups were all about the same age. This suggested that the creatures were distributed on the sea floor at the same time, indicating that they got there as either larvae or fertilised eggs floating in the current from a simultaneous spawning (where many animals release eggs and sperm into the sea at the same time to improve the chances of fertilisation taking place). Once they reached the sea floor, the primitive creatures would have fixed themselves to it, which would have prevented them from moving around to seek out a mate later in life.

They were soft-bodied creatures but are thought to have been relatively safe while swaying in the currents and tides because predators big enough to attack them had yet to evolve. Clusters of up to fifteen of the creatures were preserved because as well as being born together they probably died together when a storm whipped up the sand and smothered them.

Professor Mary Droser, of the University of California, Riverside, in the United States, identified the fossils along with James Gehling, of the South Australia Museum. She said they showed ecosystems to be complex early on in the evolution of animals and put back the history of sex by about thirty million years.

Giant Scorpion

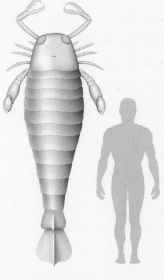

An ancient relation of spiders and scorpions bigger than a grown man has been identified as the most savage predator of its age. The sea scorpion lurked in shallow water to catch fish and other creatures which it chopped up into small pieces for easy consumption.

A 1.5ft (46cm) long claw was recovered from a quarry near Prüm in Germany and researchers calculated that the creature it came from would have been 8.2ft (2.5m) long. The fossil claw was dated to 390 million years ago and it belonged to a species of sea scorpion called *Jaekelopterus rhenania* which would have been the top predator on the planet at that time. The claw was recovered from rock formed from silt thought to have settled in a brackish lagoon or a river delta flood plain.

The species was one of the pterygotids, a group of giant sea scorpions that were at the top of the food chain for at least 37 million years. They lived in an age when arthropods, the segmented animals that today include insects, scorpions, spiders and crabs, could grow to an enormous size. Dragon-flies with wing-spans of 2.5ft (75cm) and millipedes as long as 7.5ft (2.3m) were among the giants of the era, but the biggest of all was the sea scorpion. Sea scorpions are thought to be the marine ancestors of today's land-based scorpions and possibly spiders, ticks and mites.

J. rhenania was originally described in the early twentieth century but the claw allowed researchers to reassess its potential size. The study was carried out by researchers from the University of Bristol in the UK, the German Cultural Heritage Directorate, and Yale University in the US.

above: **Reconstruction of the giant scorpion relative to the size of a human**
below: **The giant fossilised claw**

Terror of the Prehistoric Seas

A beast bigger than a humpback whale and with fangs the size of carving knives was the most fearsome reptile ever to swim in the oceans. Its jaws were so powerful that they could have crushed cars and the creature's bite is estimated to have been four times as strong as that of a *Tyrannosaurus rex*.

Analysis of the remains of a huge pliosaur have revealed that it was a turbo-charged swimmer capable of sudden surges of acceleration, which it would have used to overhaul fast prey. The marine hunter, dubbed 'Predator X', was dug up from the permafrost of Svalbard, a group of Norwegian islands in the Arctic Circle, in the summer of 2008. The vast animal was even bigger and more fearsome than a giant pliosaur nicknamed 'The Monster' that was excavated from the same location a year earlier.

Predator X lived 147 million years ago, and as one of the biggest marine predators ever to have lived, it would have been able to take on anything that moved. When alive, it would have been at least 50ft (15m) long, weighed almost 45 tons and boasted enormous flippers each measuring 10ft (3m) long.

Predator X and the slightly smaller Monster probably represent the same species of pliosaur, said Dr Jørn Hurum, of the University of Oslo Natural History Museum in Norway. He led the expeditions that uncovered both creatures, and said that their anatomy, physiology and likely hunting strategy pointed to the species being the

"most dangerous" ever to have patrolled the seas.

The turbo-charged swimming technique was pinpointed after researchers wondered why Predator X needed large flippers at both the front and the rear. Its front flippers were perfectly capable of propelling the hunter through the water at a reasonable pace, but tests using a four-flippered robot called Madeline and carried out by Dr John Long, of Vassar College in the US, revealed that the hind flippers provided the animal with the ability to surge forward at speed. Researchers believe that it would have used the front flippers to cruise through the water and would have kicked in with the hind pair when chasing prey.

The fossil remains of Predator X had broken into at least 20,000

opposite: **Artist's impression of The Monster catching a smaller plesiosaur.** above: **Size comparison – killer whale, blue whale, pliosaur (The Monster) and human diver**

clockwise from top:
The Monster; snout with collected parts highlighted, lateral view; partially reconstructed paddle; snout as reconstructed in the lab, dorsal view

allow researchers to estimate that the creature could bite down with the force of 15 tons. Dr Hurum and Dr Greg Erickson, of Florida State University in the US, calculated that the jaws were able to clamp down with four times the force of a *T. rex*'s bite and more than ten times that of an alligator, which boasts the most powerful bite of creatures alive today.

Both Predator X and The Monster would have dwarfed the average pliosaur, which were generally 16-20ft (5-6m) long with 3-4ft (0.9-1.2m) long flippers. They were half as big again as Kronosaurus, a pliosaur from Australia that was previously the biggest known. Though smaller than another ancient marine predator, a 75ft (23m) long ichthyosaur dated to 210 million years ago, their teeth were significantly bigger, which allowed them to chase larger prey. They were built for speed and savagery with a body shaped like a teardrop to minimise drag, and their 10ft long (3m) jaws bristled with an estimated 60 dagger-like teeth, many of them 12in (30cm) long.

The Monster was discovered in 2006 when its fossil bones were spotted poking from a mountainside along with the remains of dozens of other animals including another pliosaur and several ichthyosaurs. It was excavated in 2007 by a team of palaeontologists who had to keep a wary eye out for polar bears as they worked to clear away tons of shale and rock. Dr Patrick Druckenmiller, of the University of Alaska Fairbanks in Canada, was part of the team and calculated that a quarter to a third of the predator was recovered. On the last day of the expedition some large bones were seen in the earth. It was too late to dig them out but researchers made a note of the spot, taking a GPS reading to be certain. When they returned the following summer, the bones turned out to be those of Predator X.

Further evidence that the pliosaur was a top predator and a killing machine came from Dr Druckenmiller, a member of both expeditions to Svalbard. He put a pliosaur skull borrowed from the Natural History Museum in the UK into an industrial CT scanner, which revealed that the animal's brain was the same shape and, in proportion to the rest of the body, the same size as the brain of a great white shark.

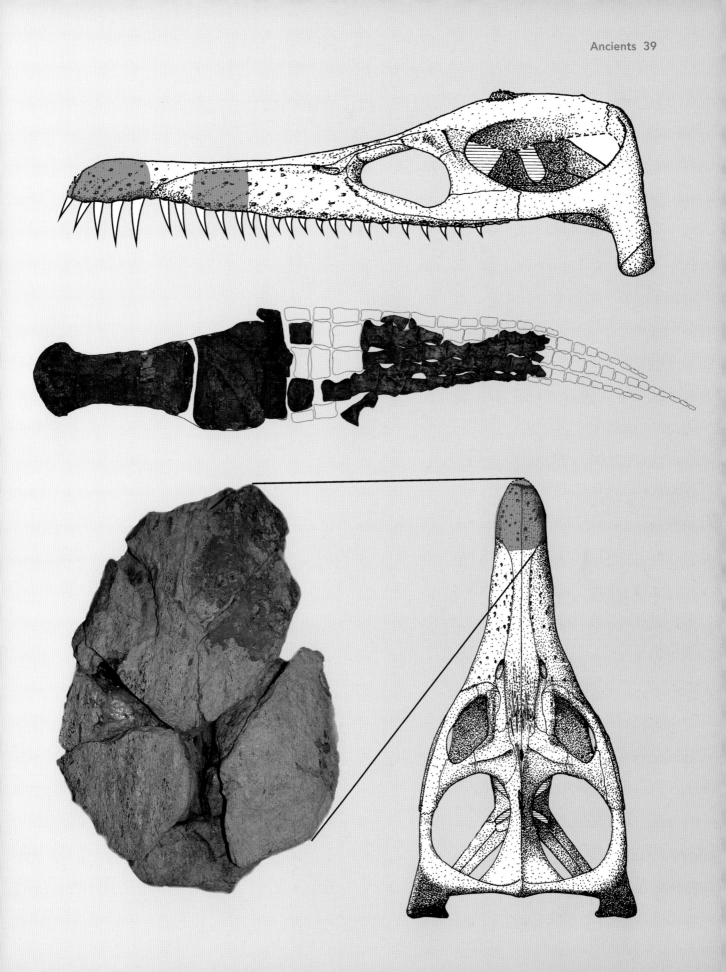

Fearsome Frog

A frog armed with teeth and big enough to prey on baby dinosaurs has provided fresh evidence on how the continents formed. The amphibian, the heaviest frog on record, was the size of a beach ball and was named the Devil's Frog by researchers impressed by its diabolic appearance. Fossilised remains of the frog, *Beelzebufo ampinga*, were found in Madagascar and were dated as 65 to 70 million years old. It was identified as a close relative of today's horned frogs, which astonished researchers because previously they had been known only in South America.

The discovery appeared incompatible with the theory that Madagascar, the Seychelles and India broke away from the Australian and Antarctic landmass 120 million years ago. An alternative theory that has been gaining support since 1927, when similarities were noted between the dinosaurs of South America, Madagascar and India, suggested that a land link had survived until much more recently. The discovery of the frog in Madagascar added considerable weight to this theory. It is uncertain why the Devil's frog died out once it reached Madagascar, but the research team of Professor Susan Evans and Dr Marc Jones of University College, London, in the UK and Dr David Krause of Stony Brook University in the US suspect that it was during a period of great change on Madagascar.

Rock deposits that held the remains of the Devil's frog show that the creature lived in much the same habitat as the South American horned frogs and would have preferred warm, dry areas with temporary pools. At up to 1.3ft (40cm) long and at around 8.8lbs (4kg) it would have dwarfed the largest horned frog alive today – the Brazilian horned frog, *Ceratophrys aurita*, can reach 4.4lbs (2kg) – but it was otherwise remarkably similar and probably hunted in much the same way.

Horned frogs are ambush specialists with a strong bite that enables them to prey on any creature they can fit into their mouths, including mice, lizards and snakes. The Devil's frog, with its squat body, large head and wide mouth, could have added newborn dinosaurs and primitive mammals to its diet.

Feather Talk

The most primitive feathers yet discovered are thought to have been used by a flightless dinosaur to communicate with mates and rivals. This early type of feather was found fossilised in rock formed from volcanic ash in the Liaoning region of China. Along with a second, more advanced type of feather, they were clearly visible on a fossilised head, neck and part of the tail of a Beipiaosaurus dinosaur. Researchers concluded the more primitive form, which grew most densely on the back of the neck and at the end of the tail, would have been best suited to signalling the animal's intentions.

Scientists had long theorised that dinosaurs could sport primitive feathers made of single filaments rather than more advanced structures with many delicate filaments, but these had not been seen until the discovery of the Beipiaosaurus. The single filaments of the primitive feather were longer and fatter than later types, and more reminiscent of a porcupine's quills than a modern bird's flight feather. They had a tubular construction and were missing the branches seen in more advanced structures.

The Liaoning discoveries were dated to 125 million years ago and bore out the argument that dinosaurs evolved the earliest type of feathers. Scientists predicted the existence of these tubular, branchless primitive feathers – called elongated broad filamentous feathers – as they were regarded as a necessary stepping stone to other types. Researchers believe the primitive feathers first appeared on animals many millions of years before the Beipiaosaurus recovered from China was walking the landscape, and in plenty of time for feathers to be inherited from dinosaurs by birds. Archaeopteryx, the earliest known feathered bird, evolved at least 147 million years ago.

Professor Xing Xu, of the Chinese Academy of Sciences, led the study and said that whilst the primitive feather would have been used for communication, the more advanced feather, which was slender and short, would have most likely provided insulation. He and his colleagues from the Chinese Academy of Geological Sciences and the Shandong Tianyu Museum of Nature said that the discovery of the feathers covering Beipiaosaurus provided further evidence that feathers evolved before either feathered flight or birds.

opposite: **Artist's impression of the Devil's frog**
right: **Reconstruction of the Beipiaosaurus displaying its feathers**

Winged Terror

Pterosaurs as tall as giraffes stalked the land in the age of the dinosaurs to snatch up prey the size of foxes and swallow them whole. The flying reptiles may have boasted wingspans that could compete with small aeroplanes but many were as at home walking on the ground as soaring in the air. Some of the biggest of all the pterosaurs were accomplished walkers and were so well adapted to living on land that they would have stalked and eaten baby dinosaurs and other animals.

A reappraisal of the fossil remains of azhdarchids, the biggest of the pterosaurs, concluded that rather than living in an aquatic environment they specialised in living inland. The largest were as tall as giraffes and had wingspans of up to 40ft (12m). Their jaws were so large that they could snap up and gulp down animals as large as modern foxes. Mark Witton and Dr Darren Naish of the University of Portsmouth in the UK have challenged the traditional idea that pterosaurs all lived either at sea or in coastal areas. They concluded that the azhdarchids were different from other pterosaurs and far from being dependent on the seas were built to be terrestrial creatures.

Rather than snatching fish from the sea while flying, or plunging their beaks into soft mud to pick out small morsels, the creatures would have snapped up prey much as storks and hornbills do today. Their limbs were long, making it likely that they were competent walkers, and their height would have helped them spy prey in the undergrowth. Their feet were too small to make them

Artist's impression of a group of giant azhdarchids. One pterosaur has grabbed a juvenile titanosaur

above: **Artist's impression of the Azhdarchid skeleton**

efficient waders or swimmers but their shape and size were ideal for wandering about on firm ground, especially their padded soles, which aided traction.

Analysis of pterosaur footprints found in South Korea indicate that they were made by an animal which was an efficient walker. They have been attributed to the species *Haenamichnus uhangriensis*, which is thought to have been an azhdarchid. The tracks were the first pterosaur footprints to be discovered in Asia and the largest anywhere. Azhdarchids, the most widespread and successful of the pterosaurs, lived from about 125 million years ago to 65.5 million years ago when they followed dinosaurs into extinction. A number of azhdarchid fossils have been found inland but it had previously been assumed that they had died while on migration rather than that they lived inland.

Another reassessment of an ancient reptile species carried out by Dr Naish and colleagues indicates that giant sauropods used to hold their necks like giraffes. At up to 100ft (30m) long and weighing as much as ten

They could snap up and gulp down animals as large as modern foxes

elephants sauropods were some of the biggest animals ever to have lived. It was originally thought that they held their necks almost horizontally but this is contradicted by the research carried out by the team that included Dr Mike Taylor from the University of Portsmouth and Dr Matt Wedel of Western University of Health Sciences in the US. Analysis of neck x-rays from ten different types of vertebrates showed that it was more likely that sauropods held their heads high. The findings indicated that the huge dinosaurs were as tall as 50ft (15m), and that a host of museum exhibits and television reconstructions have given viewers the wrong impression of sauropods.

Mighty Mouse

An enormous rodent that lived about four million years ago was at least 3,000 times bigger than a rat. The animal, *Josephoartigasia monesi*, is thought to have weighed more than a ton and was the biggest rodent yet known to have scurried – or in its case lumbered – about the landscape. It was so big that it probably spent much of its life wallowing in water, like the modern hippopotamus, to support some of its weight.

The size was calculated from a fossilised skull found in Uruguay. This allowed researchers to work out that it would have been about 10ft (3m) long and 5ft (1.5m) tall. Scientists who analysed the skull believe that even bigger specimens of up to or even exceeding 2.5 tons would have existed, making it comparable in size to modern hippos, which range from 1.4 to 3.1 tons.

The animal was dubbed Mighty Mouse and is a member of the Dinomyidae family of which there is just one survivor, the pacarana, *Dinomys branickii*. Pacaranas are among the biggest rodents alive today but at about 33lbs (15kg) are tiny in comparison to *J. monesi*. The biggest living rodent is the capybara, also from South America, which when fully grown can exceed 132lbs (60kg). Rodents make up about 40 per cent of mammals today and the vast majority weigh less than 2.2lbs (1kg). The common rat is about 0.67 lbs (0.3kg). The Mighty Mouse was just one of several giant rodents that lived in South America several million years ago. There were other giant animals too, including huge predatory birds, which would have run down and eaten the young of *J. Monesi*.

The fossil skull was analysed by Andres Rinderknecht of the National Museum of Natural History, and Dr Ernesto Blanco of the Institute of Physics, both in Uruguay. The researchers suggested that the extinct animal would have eaten mainly soft aquatic plants and fruit, but they were perplexed by its huge 12in (30cm) long incisors – a third of which were exposed – because they were much tougher than would have been expected for such a diet.

Dr Blanco said it was possible that the length and strength of the incisors was to help the animals fight off predators and courtship rivals. Equally, they could have been used to fell trees, just like a modern beaver. The estimated size of the rodent has been challenged, as only the skull of the animal had been located, but the researchers remain confident that their calculations are fair.

> It probably spent much of its life wallowing in water, like the modern hippopotamus

Titanic Snake

Giant snakes took over where dinosaurs left off by becoming the largest predators on land for at least ten million years. When dinosaurs died out they left the way open for snakes to inherit their mantle as the most fearsome beasts to rule the earth. The type of snake that became the biggest land-based predator of its era has been identified as a relative of the boa constrictor living in a primitive South American tropical rainforest. As the biggest snake of all time the animal was named Titanoboa in tribute to its extraordinary size. At least 28 examples of *Titanoboa cerrejonensis* have been recovered from an open-pit mine in Colombia and all of them were 40ft (12m) or more long.

It was estimated that the biggest of the fossilised snakes discovered at the Cerrejon Coal Mine was 42-45ft long (13-14m) and weighed 1.25 tons. It is thought likely that the species boasted some individuals much bigger than the fossilised examples recovered by researchers. By contrast, the biggest living snake is the reticulated python in South-East Asia; one 33ft (10m) long specimen has been found but, as a species, they generally grow to about 20ft (6m) long.

The fossilised remains of Titanoboa that were uncovered were dated to 58 to 60 million years ago and the snake, which was big enough to eat virtually any animal it encountered, is thought to have been king of the predators for ten million years or more. Its discovery, and the remains of some of the creatures that it would have preyed upon, are providing researchers with the most detailed picture yet of the tropical ecosystem in South America sixty million years ago.

Giant crocodile-like dryosaurs and turtles were among the creatures found fossilised in a layer of rock at the coalmine and would have been included in the snake's diet. Other fossil remains from Cerrejon that have given researchers a glimpse of the ancient landscape, the oldest known rainforest in South America, include gastropods, fish and palms. The sheer size of the snake allowed scientists to calculate that the infant rainforest ecosystem, which eventually evolved to become the Amazonian rainforest, would have been warmer than today. Researchers concluded that the tropics would, at an average of 30°C to 34°C, have been about 4°C warmer than they are today. Modern temperatures make the area too cool for a cold-blooded snake as big as Titanoboa to thrive.

As the biggest snake of all time the animal was named Titanoboa

It took several years to excavate and analyse the fossils in a joint project between the Smithsonian Tropical Research Institute in Panama, and the universities of Toronto in Canada, and Florida and Indiana in the USA. Jonathan Bloch, of the University of Florida, said the scale of Titanoboa out-stretched even the snakes of Hollywood fantasy, including the reptile that tried to eat Jennifer Lopez in the film *Anaconda*.

opposite: **A display of vertebrae and rib bones from Titanoboa.** above: **Artist's impression of Titanoboa**

Fishy Copulation

A group of primitive fish have been identified as the first backboned creatures to copulate and give birth to live offspring. It had been thought that reproduction was achieved asexually and through external fertilisation (in which sperm and eggs are released into water to mix) until the evolution of the armoured fish. But the discovery of fossilised embryos in the remains of different types of placoderms, a primitive group of fish that ruled lakes and seas for almost seventy million years, has offered new insights into the origins of sex.

In one of the fossils, that of a species called *Materpiscis attenboroughi* in honour of the naturalist Sir David Attenborough, even the umbilical cord and the egg sac were found preserved. The 10in (25cm) long female died 375 million years ago and, to the astonishment of the researchers studying the remains, an embryo about a quarter the size of the mother fish was preserved inside the body. Analysis of the mineralised umbilical cord revealed traces of tiny blood vessels, indicating that the mother fish was passing nourishment to the embryo.

It was unearthed in the Gogo area of Western Australia and was hailed as one of the most significant and extraordinary findings ever discovered by Australian palaeontologists. Dr John Long of Museum Victoria in Australia led the team that discovered the embryo, a discovery which proved that live births dated back to the earliest of the jawed vertebrates – about 200 million years earlier than had been thought.

The remains of the fish, which would have lived in a warm tropical reef system, were found in 2005 sealed within limestone that had to be slowly removed using diluted acetic acid. Once it was realised that the smaller skeleton was that of an embryo, the researchers reassessed the fossil remains of another species of placoderm, *Austroptyctodus gardineri*, which had been collected in 1986. A fresh look at the Austroptyctodus specimen by the team, which included researchers from the Australian National University and the University of Western Australia, showed that what had originally been thought to be scales were three embryos.

Further confirmation that placoderms had surprisingly advanced reproductive biology comparable to some of today's sharks and rays, was announced early in 2009 after another fossil was reassessed. This fossil, of the species *Incisoscutum ritchiei*, was also dated at 380 million years old and was again from the Gogo formation, which is thought to be the remains of an inland sea reef stretching 870 miles (1400km). Inside the fossil were the remains of a smaller fish, which when first described in the 1980s were deemed to be the larger animal's last meal. Re-examination led by Dr Long showed them to be those of an embryo.

Dr Zerina Johanson, of the Natural History Museum in the UK, said that with three placoderms known to have given birth to live offspring, it is likely that copulation was much more common from the late Silurian, 420 million years ago, to the end of the Devonian 355 million years ago, than had been suspected.

Study of male placoderms has shown that they were equipped with claspers on their pelvic fins, which in modern marine animals are used to insert a package of sperm into the female. The evolution of live birth suggests that placoderms had opted to invest a lot of energy in producing just a few well-developed offspring rather than relying on the scattergun approach of spawning.

The fossil remains of *Austroptyctodus gardineri*. What had originally thought to be scales were reinterpreted as three embryos

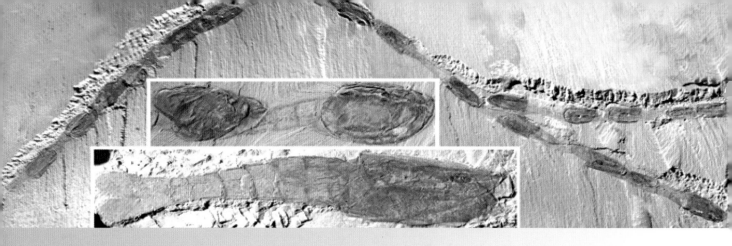

Chain Gang

Cambrian arthropod chain of shrimp-like creatures joined together

The earliest evidence of collective behaviour has been found in fossils that have frozen an ancient migration in time. Groups of a shrimp-like creature can be seen preserved in rock, still linked together 525 million years after they died. Up to twenty of the mysterious marine creatures made up each of the chains, which researchers suspect were formed to ensure safety in numbers.

An Anglo-Chinese team of researchers discovered 22 chains and one individual, which they suspect died when they entered a toxic zone in the Cambrian seas. The bodies sank to the seabed where they were covered with sediment. The animals are something of a mystery, but have been identified as early arthropods, a category that includes crustaceans, spiders and insects.

After considering various reasons for the formation of the chains, in which the lead animal's tail was inserted beneath the shell of the one behind, researchers concluded that defence during migration was the most likely. The migration might have been a daily commute when the animals rose to the surface of the sea at night to feed or it could have been a more lateral movement to a neighbouring part of the sea.

This defensive technique of joining together to travel is comparable to the trains of spiny lobsters formed today when the crustaceans protect themselves from triggerfish, though the ancient creatures were linked much more tightly.

It is unlikely that the chains were formed as part of feeding behaviour because the mouths of the creatures were covered by the tails of those in front. The research team also thought it unlikely that the chains were formed for reproductive activity because, although this does occur in modern sea squirts, there are no crustaceans alive today that display such behaviour.

How the shrimp-like animals, which were each close to an inch (2.5cm) long, swam remains a puzzle because none of the limbs or antennae that would provide clues have been preserved – assuming they existed in the first place. Professor Derek Siveter of the University of Oxford in the UK was one of the researchers who analysed the remains and he suggested that the creatures might have had a pulsating movement like salps, modern soft-bodied animals that are similar to jellyfish but form long chains in the sea.

Professor Siveter collaborated in the research project with Professors Richard Aldridge and David Siveter of the University of Leicester in the UK and Professor Xian-guang Hou of Yunnan University in China. The fossils were dug up from the Chengjiang Lagerstätte in Yunnan, an exceptionally rich deposit of fossils dating from 525 million years ago. It provides researchers with a window on life during the Cambrian Explosion when all the basic body plans of today's animals originated, together with many that were evolutionary dead ends.

Not so Bird Brained

A study of birds' brains has suggested that their superior intelligence gave them the edge that allowed them to survive the disaster that killed off the dinosaurs. Well-developed brains enabled birds to adapt to the new challenges that are thought to have ended the dinosaurs' reign 65 million years ago. Life for creatures alive during the Cretaceous-Tertiary mass extinction, which is thought most likely to have been prompted by an asteroid strike, would have been exceptionally challenging.

Researchers explained that a more advanced brain would have enabled birds to adapt better to the problems of finding food in a rapidly changing environment. CT scans of cavities in fossil skulls showed bird brains to be advanced enough to give the creatures the problem-solving skills needed to survive. A key component is probably the evolution of the wulst, a structure in the brain linked to visual perception. It is thought that the wulst evolved in modern types of birds just prior to the Cretaceous-Tertiary mass extinction, whereas it was absent in pterosaurs and the more primitive species of birds.

Dr Stig Walsh, of the Natural History Museum in the UK, said that the evolution of a bigger and more advanced brain helped explain why they survived the mass extinction, and survived to found all the avian lineages of today, when 85 per cent of animal species – including dinosaurs and pterosaurs – were wiped out. Dr Walsh and a colleague, Dr Angela Milner, reached their conclusions after analysing the brain cavities of Archaeopteryx, a primitive bird dated to 147 million years ago, and two marine species dated to 55 million years ago.

Archaeopteryx lacked the wulst and was found to have a much more limited brain than those of the other two species, *Odontopteryx toliapica* and *Prophaethon shrubsolei*, which are close relations of today's frigate birds, albatrosses, storm petrels and pelicans.

The mental capacity of the two marine birds, which had the wulst, was found to be just as advanced as those of today's birds in controlling the ability to learn, sight and flight. CT scanning provided such precise three-dimensional images of the brain cavity that it was even possible for the researchers to pick out the shape of nerves. The study was limited to three skulls because few have survived in good enough condition to reveal the shape and size of the brain.

> The evolution of a bigger brain helped explain why the birds survived the mass extinction

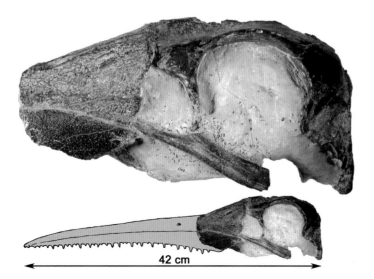

42 cm

left: **The skull of Dasornis showing the fossil specimen and a reconstruction of the complete skull**
below: **Artist's reconstruction of a giant pseudo-toothed bird**

Mother Goose with Teeth

A giant goose-like bird with a beakful of teeth that dipped and soared in the air 50 million years ago was the albatross of its day. It boasted a span of 16ft (5m) from wingtip to wingtip, making it almost as big as a light aircraft and almost fifty per cent bigger than the wandering albatross, the bird with the biggest wingspan today.

Despite its size and the discovery that its closest relatives, either living or extinct, are ducks and geese, the biggest surprise provided by the huge bird, dubbed Mother Goose, was the teeth. Birds dispensed with teeth about 100 million years ago, but they re-evolved 50 million years later in bony form in *Dasornis emuinus*.

Instead of the enamel and dentine found in other animals' teeth, those of Mother Goose were made of bone and, perhaps, coated with keratin, the same material found in beaks. Researchers suspect the 60-80 "pseudo-teeth" along the cutting edges of the beak evolved to help it grip slippery prey such as squid and fish.

> The pseudo-teeth along the cutting edges of the beak evolved to help it grip slippery prey

It is thought that it filled a similar ecological niche to today's albatrosses, flying huge distances over the oceans and snapping up prey from the surface waters. Rather than flap its wings all the time to remain airborne– an exhausting process – it probably glided for most of the time making maximum use of thermals. It would have cruised over the seas covering what is now south-eastern Britain, and when it died, it sank to the bottom to be covered in sediment.

D. emuinus was identified from the fossilised remains of a skull by Dr Gerald Mayr, of the Senckenberg Research Institute and Natural History Museum in Frankfurt, Germany. The skull was originally found in clay on the Isle of Sheppey, in the United Kingdom, by a private collector. Close analysis of the well-preserved skull meant, said Dr Mayr, that the list of species of giant bony-toothed birds needed reassessing. He maintained that remains previously identified as three other species of giant, bony-toothed birds should be reassigned as *D. emuinus*.

Darwin's Missing Link

A fossilised animal with the head of a seal and a body like an otter has provided the first solid support for a theory put forward by Charles Darwin 150 years ago. The carnivorous mammal is the most primitive ancestor of seals, sealions and walruses yet found, and was primarily a freshwater rather than a marine animal.

Darwin suggested in 1859 that the ancestors of seals first took to the water in rivers and lakes rather than the sea. In *On the Origin of Species* he wrote: "A strictly terrestrial animal, by occasionally hunting for food in shallow water, then in streams or lakes, might at last be converted into an animal so thoroughly aquatic as to brave the open ocean."

Until the discovery of the fossil remains in 2007 and 2008 at Devon Island in Nunavut, Canada, there was little to back the idea of freshwater origins. But the 3ft (1m) long animal, named *Puijila darwini*, was found in rock formed by sediment at the bottom of a freshwater Arctic lake close to the coast. Researchers who analysed the remains believe that the animal, which, like its modern relatives, is classed as a pinniped relied on the lake for food. However, the climate in the area meant that there was a risk the lake would freeze over during the winter, which researchers believe would have

It had the body of a modern day otter and was described as a "walking seal"

forced the animal to move temporarily to the sea to seek prey. *Puijila darwini* was hailed as a missing link in the pinnipid lineage because it was the earliest aquatic member. It had yet to develop flippers but a feature of its skeleton – the flattened finger and toe bones – suggested it had webbed feet to help propel it through the water. With a body resembling a modern-day otter's, it is thought to have been a capable swimmer and would have paddled with its front and hind legs. Its heavy, muscular limbs would have enabled it to walk comfortably on land, and it was described as a "walking seal" by Dr. Natalia Rybczynski of the Canadian Museum of Nature, who uncovered and analysed the fossil with Dr Mary Dawson, of the Carnegie Museum of Natural History, and Dr Richard Tedford of the American Museum of Natural History, both in the US.

The animal's discovery in Devon Island provided long-sought evidence that pinnipeds evolved in the Arctic – an idea that had fallen out of favour because of lack of evidence. Until Puijila was discovered, the earliest aquatic pinniped was Enaliarctos, which dates from about the same time, but had flippers, and was found on the Pacific shores of North America. The fossil was named Puijila, which means "young sea mammal" in the language of the Inuit people in Nunavut, and darwini in honour of Darwin.

The lake the animal swam in when alive formed in a crater left by a meteorite and the sedimentary rock where the fossil was found has yielded many other finds in the last thirty years. Among the animals that would have lived in the same cool, temperate environment was a small but powerful rhinoceros, shrews, rabbits, a bird similar to a swan, and a deer-like animal. In the water were several types of fish including a trout and a smelt-like species. Alder and larches would have been the most common trees; others that Puijila is likely to have encountered are chestnuts, sweetgum, birch, pine, fir, and spruce.

Skeletal reconstruction of *Puijila darwini*, the walking seal

Head Butting Dinosaur

A huge predatory dinosaur has been discovered which is thought to have fought for mating rights by head-butting its rivals. The dinosaur, which lived 110 million years ago, had prominent bony brows and other stress-absorbing features, which scientists believe allowed the animals to smash their heads together in a test of strength. The thick, hard brows, which were probably covered in keratin for extra toughness, would have been the equivalent 110 million years ago of the antlers and horns grown by animals today. The ridges on its face would have given the creature, the top predator of its day, an especially fierce appearance. It was named *Eocarcharia dinops*, meaning "fierce-eyed dawn shark", in recognition of its appearance, its armoury of sharp teeth and its role as ancestor to some of the biggest predators ever to walk.

Analysis of the fossil remains was carried out by Professor Paul Sereno of the University of Chicago in the US and Steve Brusatte of the University of Bristol in the UK who found that its teeth were ideally suited to killing and tearing apart prey. They concluded that Eocarcharia was the earliest known member of a group of dinosaurs called charodontosaurids, which were the top predators on the southern super-continent Gondwana. Among the beasts to follow it were Gigantosaurus and Mapusaurus, which were as big, or bigger, than *Tyrannosaurus rex*, a species that was restricted to the northern continents. The researchers calculated that Eocarcharia was 20-26ft (6-8m) long and ran on its hind legs.

Remains of the dinosaur were dug up from the Sahara desert and were found in the same rock formation as the fossilised bones of the two other meat-eaters that would have joined it in a terrifying triumvirate that dominated the environment. One of the other creatures was *Suchomimus tenerensis*, a previously identified species which caught and ate mostly fish. The third was a hunter that was similar in size to Eocarcharia and also unknown to science. All three had short forelimbs and used their muscular back legs for running.

Palaeontologists named the second unknown dinosaur *Kryptops palaios*, meaning "old hidden face", because it had a horny covering over most of its face. The design of Kryptops indicated that it was a meat-eater, but rather than rushing around after live prey it is thought that it was primarily a scavenger, using its short but sharp teeth to rip off mouthfuls from carcasses.

Stress-absorbing features allowed the animals to smash their heads together

According to Mr Brusatte, the three meat-eaters would have had different roles and food sources in the environment 110 million years ago, just as lions, cheetahs and hyenas do today. Kryptops, he suggested, would have filled a niche similar to that of the hyena. It was about 20-23ft (6-7m) long and is thought to have been the first of the abelisaurids, a group of carnivores that went on to dominate what is today India and South America.

Other remains located in the same rock formation at Gado-ufaoua in Niger's Ténéré Desert, part of the Sahara, included some of the species that the newly discovered dinosaurs would have eaten. Among them were the long-necked plant-eater *Nigersaurus taqueti* and several crocodile-like creatures.

opposite: *Kryptops palaios* had a horny covering over most of its face
below: *Eocarcharia dinops* had a particularly fierce appearance

Back to the Drawing Board

One of the first birds to take to the air exhibited a design fault that made it liable to fall out of trees. Eoconfuciusornis lived 131 million years ago and was capable of flying, but would have struggled to grip the tree branches it rested on. It would have been adept at climbing up into the trees, probably both to seek food and to give it height to launch into the air, but because of the way its claws were configured sitting on a branch and landing comfortably posed problems.

Sitting on a branch and landing comfortably posed problems

The only bird to predate it was Archaeopteryx, which has been dated to 147 million years ago, though Eoconfuciusornis was the first toothless bird. An astonishingly well-preserved fossil, which included the remains of feathers, revealed it to be about the size of a modern rook. By contrast with modern birds it would have been a slow, inefficient flier, but its evolution marked a great advance in flying ability. Whereas Archaeopteryx could probably only manage a distance of about a mile before it needed to rest, Eoconfuciusornis could have confidently flown several miles.

The 131 million-year-old bird was unearthed in the Dabeigou Formation at Sichakou in the Hebei Province of northern China. It was named *Eoconfuciusornis zhengi* in honour of Guangmei Zheng, a Chinese ornithologist. Its discovery helped fill a thirty million year gap in the understanding of avian evolution between Archaeopteryx and other primitive birds from the Early Cretaceous. Analysis showed it to be the earliest and most primitive of the Confuciusornithids, which were previously thought to be only 120 to 125 million years old.

Professor Michael Benton, of the University of Bristol in the UK, along with Dr Fucheng Zhang and Dr Zhonghe Zhou of the Chinese Academy of Sciences in Beijing, described the fossilised remains in 2008. Among the differences between Eoconfuciusornis and modern birds was the structure of the upper fore-limb, which showed it to be a much weaker flier. Nevertheless, said Professor Benton, for its time it would have been advanced and even though it occasionally fell from trees it would have been well adapted to its environment. "No one said evolution had to be perfect," he said. "Just good enough."

The fossilised bird is thought to have died while flying over a shallow lake; or it might have fallen into the water and been unable to get out again. The near-complete skeleton indicated that fish and other aquatic creatures had not been able to scavenge the remains, suggesting that the lake was probably stagnant at the time the bird died.

opposite: **The fossilised bird with feathers still intact**
above: **Reconstruction of Eoconfuciusornis**

Jigsaw Puzzle Killer

It grabbed its prey
with two primitive
claws then used its
teeth like a grinder

A bizarre and mysterious animal that was less than two feet long has been identified as a super-predator. When *Hurdia victoria* swam through the seas more than 500 million years ago it was about as deadly as predators came. It had eyes on stalks, similar to those of flies today, that were the last word in vision when it was alive.

Gills were arrayed in rows along more than half its body-length; it had an armoured front section and its mouth was equipped with rows of teeth arranged so that it could grind through the hard shells of its prey. But its design was so odd that it has taken a century for palaeontologists studying its fossil remains to ascertain what it looked like.

More than 500 fossils of the marine killer have been found but almost all were disassembled, and even the handful of more complete specimens were difficult to interpret. Since 1912, when it was first held to be a

Artist's reconstruction
of *Hurdia victoria*

it has been variously described as a jellyfish and a sea cucumber. Scientists have discounted some of the remains as those of different animals and are now convinced that they have reassembled the remaining disarticulated fossil pieces correctly and that they belong to *H. victoria*.

The animal that has been revealed was one of the top predators of its age, able to swim after and catch prey. The more complete fossils show animals up to 8in (20cm) long but disarticulated pieces suggest it could grow to 2ft (50cm). Despite its small size, it would have been the Cambrian equivalent of the top killers that evolved later, such as the great white shark. Fossil remains have been found across wide parts of North America and China and so it would have been widespread and, in all likelihood, a hunter able to prey on a wide variety of species.

Dr Greg Edgecombe, of the UK's Natural History Museum, described it as a bizarre creature and said that its mouth, consisting of 32 plates with circular rows of teeth within, was one of its more extraordinary features. It grabbed its prey with two primitive claws close to its mouth, then used its teeth like a grinder to cut its way through the hard shells of prey such as trilobites. Other features of its body are still shrouded in mystery, including the profusion of gills along more than half of its length and the purpose of the three-part shell structure in front of its mouth.

Allison Daley, of Uppsala University in Sweden, spent three years studying the animal's remains for her doctoral thesis, and said that the carapace structure at the front of the predator's body was unlike anything seen in other animals, either alive or extinct. The carapace was fairly hard, similar to a centipede's firm exterior, but what it was and why the thin armour did not extend further along the body remains to be answered.

Miniature Dinosaurs

Fossils which lay unnoticed in a museum drawer for a quarter of a century are forcing palaeontologists to reassess their ideas about ecosystems in the age of dinosaurs. The fossilised remains are those of an extinct animal, smaller than a modern pet cat, which has been identified as the tiniest dinosaur yet uncovered in North America. *Hesperonychus elizabethae* was equipped with sharp teeth and vicious claws, but rather than ripping chunks out of huge, lumbering herbivores it was more likely to have feasted on insects, amphibians and small mammals.

Until it was discovered by researchers from the University of Calgary in Canada, carnivorous dinosaurs of such a small scale were absent from the fossil record in North America. The smallest on record was the size of a modern day wolf. Palaeontologists are now having to re-evaluate the role of carnivorous dinosaurs in the ecosystem because, while Hesperonychus was small, it appears from the many fossil remains attributed to it, that the mini-dinosaur once existed in large numbers. One of the puzzles before its discovery, said Dr Nick Longrich of the University of Calgary, was why small meat-eating dinosaurs were completely absent from the fossil record when today's large predators are vastly outnumbered by tiny hunters.

The identification of Hesperonychus raises the possibility that there were many more tiny dinosaurs scurrying through the undergrowth and that they were a much bigger part of the ancient environment than had been suspected. Hesperonychus lived in the swamps and forests of North America 75 million years ago. It ran on two legs, weighed about 4.4lbs (2kg) and would have been about 20in (50cm) tall. It resembled, and was closely related to, Velociraptor but was built on a much smaller scale.

Fossilised remains from the dinosaur were collected from the Dinosaur Park Formation in Alberta, Canada in 1982

Artist's reconstruction of Hesperonychus

by the late Dr Elizabeth Nichols, of the Royal Tyrrell Museum, Canada. The fossils were initially interpreted as coming from juvenile dinosaurs, but when Dr Longrich came across them in the University of Alberta's collection in 2007 they were reclassified. He and his colleague, Dr Philip Currie of the University of Alberta, became convinced the fossils represented a mini dinosaur when they studied a pelvis and found it had been fused to the hip bones during the animal's life; a sure sign that it had reached adulthood before it died.

Until the discovery of Hesperonychus the smallest dinosaur in North America was *Albertonykus borealis*, a chicken-sized dinosaur which ran on two legs and which was found by Dr Longrich and Dr Currie in another collaboration. It was dated as seventy million years old. Analysis of the forelimbs led the scientists to conclude that the slender creature is likely to have specialised in eating termites or other insects. Its forearms, like the rest of it, were small, but in proportion to its body they were more powerful than those of a *Tyrannosaurus rex*. The arms seemed ideally suited to digging but they were thought too short to be those of a burrowing animal. Instead, it was thought they were likely to have been used for tearing logs apart in search of insects.

Fossil bones from Albertonykus were excavated by Dr Currie at Dry Island Buffalo Jump Provincial Park in 2002 but were left in storage until it was decided to compare them to Albertosaurus, a type of tyrannosaur.

The Land Whale

A fossilised pregnant whale has been identified as an ancient species that had to return to land to give birth. The mother whale was close to full term when she died 47.5 million years ago and the calf was almost three feet long. Analysis of the remains has shown that the whale, *Maiacetus inuus*, was an early type still tied to the land.

The design of its strong, flipper-like legs suggests that it would have slept and bred on land while leading a semi-aquatic life. Its limbs were strong enough to support its weight but only for short periods and distances, so it is unlikely that it could have strayed far from the shore. Sharp, well-developed teeth in the calf indicate that it would have been able to defend itself from predators while waiting for its mother to return to the beach from hunting expeditions at sea.

The mother and unborn calf, a previously unknown species, were discovered in 2000 in the Kunvit area of Pakistan, and in 2004 an even better preserved male was excavated. Although the male was 8.5ft (2.6m) long (12 per cent bigger than the female), it is thought he was too small to have been able to command a harem. Studies of modern animals, such as sealions, have shown that males have to be at least 16 per cent larger than the females to be able to form and defend a harem.

Researchers from Pakistan, Germany and the US were involved in the discovery and analysis of the remains. They concluded the whale was a protocetid, one of the earliest types of whale. Professor Philip Gingerich, of the University of Michigan in the US, said the remains were so complete they were the fossil equivalent of the Rosetta Stone because so much detail about the creatures' lives and evolution could be read.

When the mother whale died the calf was positioned for a head-first delivery, indicative of a land birth, rather than tail-first which is typical of fully-aquatic mammals. The early female whale came to rest belly up on the sea floor, much like many other early whales detected in the fossil record. It is thought that gases building up in the stomach as a result of decomposition led to this position.

> The whale slept and bred on land while leading a semi-aquatic life

When no Bird Sang

Archaeopteryx, the earliest known bird, would have struggled to hear the alarm calls and complex singing that are commonplace among modern species. Measurements of its inner ear have revealed that it was equipped to hear only deep and low-pitched sounds, leaving it deaf to any others. Because low-pitched sounds travel better in areas of dense vegetation, this finding adds to the evidence that the proto-bird would have been primarily a forest species.

Computed tomography (CT) imaging of a fossil skull of *Archaeopteryx lithographica* was used to provide a three-dimensional picture of the proto-bird's inner ear. The cochlea duct (the bony part of the inner ear which contains the hearing organ) was shown by the scans to be relatively short, indicating a creature that heard only low-pitched sounds. Researchers studying animal ears have found that the length of the cochlea is linked to the range of sounds that can be picked up. Creatures with shorter cochleas struggle to detect medium and high-pitched sounds.

Dr Stig Walsh, of the Natural History Museum in Britain, suspected that the hearing range shown by the scans indicated that Archaeopteryx would have been able to make sounds when it was alive 147 million years ago, but would have been limited to "a low chortle" rather than complex melodies. The detectable sound range indicated for the ancient bird by the CT scans averaged 2,000Hz, giving it better hearing than its reptilian relatives such as the modern-day skink, which has an average of 400Hz, but putting it far behind the 20,000Hz boasted by humans. The three-dimensional images showed that its hearing was within the ranges displayed by modern birds but that its limitations would have put it towards the bottom of the pile. Its hearing range would have compared to that of the emu, which among modern birds is regarded as among the hardest of hearing. By contrast, the predatory barn owl has an average range of 8,000Hz, which helps it pinpoint prey in the dark.

Lawrence Witmer, of Ohio University in the US, says that using CT scans to reveal the shape of the inner ear of other extinct animals will help scientists glean insights into their habitat preferences, how sociable they were, and how complex their calls were. Previous estimates of the hearing capacity of extinct animals could only be made by looking at their brain sizes and comparing them to modern counterparts. To assess the link between hearing and cochlea duct length the research team from the Natural History Museum, Ohio University, and the Technical University of Munich in Germany, looked at 59 species of animals including turtles, crocodiles, birds, lizards and beak-headed reptiles.

> It would have struggled to hear the alarm calls and complex singing of modern species

Mammoth Hunter

A fearsome bone-crushing wolf which brought down and killed mammoths was driven into extinction because its prey disappeared. When a range of large prey species died out at the end of the last Ice Age the eastern Beringian grey wolf followed them into oblivion.

The pack hunter specialised in bringing down large prey such as mammoths, bison, horses, caribou, yak and woodland musk ox, which were all capable of inflicting serious or fatal injuries on their attackers. To help it grapple with its prey and to tear apart their carcasses the carnivore, which lived in Alaska in the US, developed a tougher skull and teeth than modern grey wolves. The adaptations meant that the wolf had a more forceful bite than modern wolves and ensured it was perfectly equipped to rip flesh from carcasses and crunch up bones. The ability to shatter the bones, much as modern spotted hyenas do, is thought to have helped the wolves ensure that little of a kill went to waste. Making the most of a meal would have been essential because there was stiff competition for food from large predators such as sabre-tooth cats, short-faced bears, and American lions.

Analysis revealed that the predator's teeth were generally more worn and more likely to have been broken than those of other grey wolves. The condition of the teeth indicated that the eastern Beringian grey wolves relied much more on chewing the bones of prey than do modern wolves in North America. Incisors and carnassial teeth were particularly vulnerable, which suggested the wolves used them for gnawing in the same way as modern spotted hyenas. Although they were capable of catching and dismembering large prey they probably scavenged when the opportunity arose.

The eastern Beringian grey wolf was a type of grey wolf, *Canis lupus*, but was genetically distinct from the predators found in North America today. Researchers were able to analyse and compare mitochondrial DNA of eastern Beringian grey wolves and other grey wolves, both modern and contemporary, and were surprised to find that there appears to be an absence of interbreeding. The eastern Beringian variety died out at the end of the Pleistocene epoch about 12,000 years ago without leaving any of its genetic heritage in the modern wolves that moved into its Alaskan territory after its extinction.

By measuring the isotopic values in the bones of eastern Beringian wolves the research team, led by scientists from the University of California, Los Angeles in the US, were able to establish that the predators ate a variety of species, some of which, like mammoths, died out at the end of the Pleistocene. The identification of a previously unrecognised type of grey wolf in Alaska during the Late Pleistocene, which lasted from 126,000 years ago to just under 12,000 years ago, suggests that more animals with special adaptations but without qualifying as fully separate species may have gone extinct at the end of the epoch than had been realised.

> The wolf was perfectly equipped to rip flesh from carcasses and crunch up bones

A modern day grey wolf, *Canis lupus*

Extinction Threats

On a Road to Nowhere

Animals and plants are being lost at such a rate that the modern era is already being described as the sixth great extinction period. The fossil record has revealed that five great extinction periods have taken place, including the Cretaceous-Tertiary extinction event that saw the dinosaurs die out. The dinosaurs are thought to have been lost after an asteroid slammed into the planet 65.5 million years ago. Volcanic activity is suspected to have played a leading role in the Permian-Triassic extinction event 251.4 million years ago, but today's extinctions are largely attributed to man's influence. Pollution, climate change, habitat destruction, and hunting are among the factors that have taken and continue to take an enormous toll on the world's wildlife

Interior Townsend's

Coastal Townsend's

Hybrid zones

Hermit

Sex as a Weapon

A bird is driving a sister species into oblivion by seducing its females and beating up any of the males who object. Townsend's warblers are more aggressive and better brawlers than their hermit warbler cousins and take full advantage in the breeding season. They drive away the male hermits and mate with the females, creating a large population of hybrid birds on the frontline between the territories of the two species. Because the more aggressive species is similarly able to out-compete the hybrid birds, the eventual descendants – bar the remnants of mitochondrial DNA bequeathed by the female hermits – are Townsend's warblers.

Hermit warblers have so far been driven out of territory stretching at least 1,200 miles along the North American West Coast and appear helpless in the face of the onslaught. They are still a common bird on the West Coast but genetic analysis has revealed that they are being driven into extinction. The process, revealed by researchers from the University of Washington in the US, offers scientists a rare glimpse of natural extinction in action. Townsend's warblers, said Meade Krosby, one of the researchers, were "brutes" which "just smacked the hermit warblers out of the way."

Hermit and Townsend's warblers shared a common ancestor about 400,000 years ago when they split to become two similar but distinct species. Each had much the same lifestyle, both living in forests, but while the hermit warblers inhabited coastal zones, the Townsend's warbler was confined to inland areas

> Townsend's warblers are more aggressive and better brawlers than their hermit cousins

cut off from the Pacific Ocean by mountains. Once the last Ice Age ended about 12,000 years ago it became possible for the Townsend's warbler to start expanding its range northwards and when it reached British Columbia it passed the northerly limit of the mountains that separated the two species. About 5,000 years ago it was able to move westwards into the territory of the hermit warbler in Alaska and British Columbia, and since then has been pushing southwards along the west coasts of Canada and the US.

The progression towards extinction was revealed by traces of hermit DNA in the Townsend's warblers living in coastal zones. Such remnants were not present in Townsend's warblers living in their traditional inland territories. The hybrid zone is found today in the states of Oregon and Washington but it is gradually moving southwards as the Townsend's take over. Unless the hermits are able to stage a comeback it is expected that they will be driven further south until the last of them disappears from California, the southern limit of their range today. They are estimated to have less than 5,000 years left. Dr Krosby carried out the study with Dr Joshua Tewksbury and said that the DNA evidence offers scientists a signal revealing natural extinctions in progress. Natural extinctions are known to have taken place many times but have proved difficult to identify.

opposite: **Hermit warbler (top) and Townsend's warbler. Map showing the hermit breeding range in light grey and the Townsend's in dark grey. Coloured lines encircle the three populations under analysis: coastal Townsend's in yellow, interior Townsend's in red and hermit in blue**

The Last Emperors

Emperor penguins, the stars of two Oscar-winning films, are threatened with a catastrophic slump in numbers by the end of the century. Sea ice is retreating at such a rate that researchers have calculated there is a serious risk that the penguin will suffer a 95 per cent crash in its population by 2100. Researchers reached this conclusion after taking into account the joint impacts of fluctuations in the sea ice coverage and long term climate change on the species. Using mathematical models the French and US team calculated that there was a 36 to 80 per cent chance of the penguins losing 95 per cent of their population – a cut that would make extinction likely.

Researchers were able to check their forecast against detailed data collected since the 1960s on a colony of emperor penguins at Terre Adélie in Antarctica. Fluctuations in the sea ice coverage are known to affect emperor penguin numbers, and one sudden fluctuation in the 1970s caused the Terre Adélie population to fall by half. The impacts over the century are expected to reduce the colony's numbers from 3,000 breeding pairs to just 400 breeding pairs at the very least and it could easily be worse. If the effects are replicated in other parts of Antarctica, and if the penguins continue to show an inability to adapt to changing

Sea ice is retreating at such a rate that there is a serious risk the Emperor penguin will suffer a 95 per cent crash in its population by 2100

Juvenile Emperor penguins

conditions, the species is likely to be on the brink of extinction in less than a hundred years.

Sea ice is important to emperor penguins, the stars of the 2005 documentary film *March of the Penguins* and the 2006 animated film *Happy Feet*, because it is where they incubate their eggs and raise their young. The absence or early break-up of sea ice also increases the chances that food will be in short supply because it reduces the quantity of krill, which are a vital food for the fish the penguin eats. Previous studies have established that when sea ice coverage is at a low level emperor penguin survival rates fall.

The research was a joint project between scientists from the Expéditions Polaires Françaises and Institut Paul Émile Victor based in France and the Woods Hole Ocean Oceanographic Institution, the National Center for Atmospheric Research, and the National Snow and Ice Data Center in the US. A report issued by WWF indicates that the species has already suffered serious population falls over the last fifty years. At the Pointe Géologie colony the numbers of emperor penguins have halved. Warming on Antarctica's western Peninsula has taken place up to five times faster than in other parts of the globe and there is increasing confidence among scientists that it is part of a global warming trend rather than a

localised anomaly. The WWF have cited overfishing as another dangerous threat to emperors, *Aptenodytes forsteri*.

Northern rockhopper penguins, *Eudyptes moseleyi*, are another species in decline and they are disappearing from UK Overseas Territory at the rate of a hundred a day. It is estimated that two million northern rockhoppers have vanished from Tristan da Cunha and Gough Island in the South Atlantic over the last fifty years. On Gough it took just 45 years for the population to crash by 90 per cent. A similar proportion disappeared over 130 years on Tristan da Cunha, 230 miles (370km) away. On its two other strongholds – the French-administered St Paul and Amsterdam Islands in the Indian Ocean – there is a similar decline.

Conservationists assessing the problem have been unable to pinpoint the cause of the slump, though they suspect that climate change and overfishing are to blame. Richard Cuthbert, of the Royal Society for the Protection of Birds, was involved in the study of northern rockhoppers on Tristan da Cunha and Gough and fears that the species is "sliding towards oblivion". The penguin has been classed as endangered and it is down from historically vast numbers to an estimated 32,000 to 65,000 pairs on Gough and 40,000 to 50,000 pairs on Tristan da Cunha.

Poached to Death

Northern white rhinos have been declared extinct in the wild with the last four remaining animals feared to have fallen prey to poachers. The four animals lived in the Garamba National Park in the Democratic Republic of Congo, but in 2008 it was concluded that they had become victims of the rise of poachers, prompted by war and civil unrest. Only a handful of the northern white rhinos, *Ceratotherium simum cottoni*, remain in captivity, but the animals are so difficult to breed and exist in such low numbers that the sub-species is regarded as doomed.

The rhinos had been in desperate trouble since the 1970s when numbers fell from 500 to fifteen, and despite a slight rise to thirty in 2003, by 2006 there were only four left. It was one of five recognised sub-species of rhino remaining in Africa. A sixth, the West African black rhino, *Diceros bicornis longipes*, was declared extinct in 2006 after an intensive search of its last refuges in northern Cameroon failed to pinpoint a single one.

A handful remain in captivity but exist in such low numbers that the sub-species is regarded as doomed

Hope for other rhinos, however, has improved quite a bit, according to surveys overseen by the International Union for Conservation of Nature (IUCN). Despite the loss of one of the sub-species, the overall numbers of the critically endangered black rhino, *Diceros bicornis*, rose from 3,730 in 2005 to 4,180 in 2007. They are found mainly in South Africa, Namibia, Zimbabwe and Kenya but are increasingly spreading across borders into neighbouring countries. Conservationists have also been encouraged by the rise in the number of Southern white rhinos, *Ceratotherium simum simum*, from 14,540 in 2005 to 17,480 in 2007.

Northern white rhino, now declared extinct in the wild

End of the Line

The last female descendant of a group of reptiles that scampered beneath the feet of dinosaurs could be born by the end of the century. Global warming threatens to wipe out the two remaining species of tuataras because their gender is directly linked to the temperature of the eggs. Alien species in their native New Zealand have driven them from most of their territory over the last two centuries, and they are now restricted to a few islands. With such a limited range the reptiles cannot lay their eggs in the cooler regions that would guarantee them a good mix of male and female offspring. Instead, by the mid 2080s, rising temperatures could mean that the last ever female tuatara will be born, unless the animals can adapt their behaviour or are helped by humans.

The tuatara's gender is directly linked to the temperature of the eggs

The temperature determines whether a clutch of eggs will result in the offspring being all male, all female, or a mix of the two. If eggs are kept below 21.2°C the hatchlings will all be female, and if the temperature is above 22.25°C they will all be male. Anything in between will result in a mix of males and females. By 2085, however, global warming could force temperatures in New Zealand to rise by up to 4°C, which would be high enough to ensure that all of the newborn North Brother Island tuataras, *Sphenodon guntheri*, are male.

The second, more numerous species, the Cook Strait tuatara, *S. Punctatus*, is expected to have slightly longer, though the last of the females could be born before 2100. Complete extinction would take several decades longer as tuataras have been known to live for more than a hundred years, although sixty is more usual.

Tuataras always nest in open areas and, researchers have concluded, unless they adapt by choosing more shaded and cooler places to lay their eggs, they will need human help to escape extinction. Using shade to ensure that eggs stay cool would be one option; another would be to move some of the reptiles to new locations once the sites have been cleared of alien species such as rats. The North Brother Island species occurs naturally only on the island from which it takes its name, but has been successfully introduced to three other small islands. The prospects of the reptile were assessed in a study by researchers from the University of Western Australia and the University of Melbourne in Australia, the University of Wellington in New Zealand, and the University of Wisconsin in the US.

Tuataras are the last members of an order of reptiles, the Sphenodontids, which evolved 220 million years ago. They grow to about 2ft long (60cm), weigh 2.2lbs (1kg) and are similar enough in body shape to their ancestors to have been dubbed "living fossils". They look like lizards, in particular iguanas, but are distinct from them in several ways. Among the odd features boasted by tuataras are the ability to hold their breath for an hour, the lack of a penis, the lack of external ears and the possession of a "third eye". The function of the third eye, which has a lens and retina, has yet to be explained as it is hidden beneath scales. Researchers suspect that it helps the animals, which despite being cold-blooded are largely nocturnal, to know the time of day.

The Cook Strait tuatara, one of the two remaining species, is threatened with extinction

Death by Tourism

The Madeiran large white disappeared almost without anyone noticing

The demand for holiday homes has been cited as one of the prime factors in driving a butterfly into extinction. Madeiran large whites lived, as their name suggests, on the Portuguese island of Madeira in the Atlantic Ocean.

A fifteen-year search was carried out in the hope of uncovering a surviving colony, but in 2007 it was named as the first of Europe's butterflies to become extinct as a direct result of human activities. Pollution from agricultural fertilisers is thought to have played a role in its demise, but the main factor in pushing it into extinction was the construction of homes for both islanders and the seven million foreign visitors who arrive each year.

It was declared dead at a butterfly conservation conference held in Laufen, Germany, amid warnings that other European species could soon follow it into oblivion. Little was known about the habits and needs of the butterfly, *Pieris wollastoni*, beyond the fact it was found mostly in north-facing valleys in the Laurisilva, a type of laurel forest. Martin Warren, of Butterfly Conservation in the UK, carried out an assessment of the threat posed to the species in 2000 with Chris van Swaay, of the Dutch Butterfly Foundation, and said that the Madeiran large white had disappeared almost without anyone noticing.

The extinct butterfly
Madeiran Large White

Into the Frying Pan

Primates in tropical forests are being eaten into extinction by people in parts of Africa and Asia, where they are hunted and served up as nutritious dishes. Large primates such as howler monkeys, red colobuses, mangabeys and langurs are among the favourite species – at 10 to 20lbs each (4.5 to 9kg) they provide plenty of meat.

Conservationists who carried out an assessment of primate populations around the world were surprised at the extent of the damage being caused by hunting. Habitat loss remains the single biggest factor in driving primates into extinction, but hunting by humans has been identified as a significant additional cause.

Kirk's red colobus in Tanzania and Zanzibar, L'Hoest's monkey and the golden monkey in Rwanda, and Delacour's langur and the Tonkin snub-nosed monkey in Vietnam are among the primates most likely to go into the cooking pot. Primates are among the easiest animals for human hunters to catch in tropical forests because they make calls which draw attention to themselves in the tree canopy, and they are relatively easy to spot.

Of the 634 species of primate, excluding man, 303 are under threat and 69 are critically endangered. Cambodia presents the worst statistics, as 90 per cent of primates are threatened with extinction. Overall in Asia, 71 per cent are at risk. Red colobus monkeys in Africa are under particular pressure with eleven classified as endangered or critically endangered. Conservationists fear that two species are already extinct: no one has seen Bouvier's red colobus, *Piliocolobus pennantii bouvieri*, for twenty-five

> ## Primates are among the easiest animals for human hunters to catch

years, and there have been no confirmed sightings of Miss Waldron's red colobus, *Piliocolobus badius waldroni*, since 1978.

Despite the gloomy assessment for many primate species in the 2008 review carried out for the International Union for Conservation of Nature (IUCN), there were some encouraging findings. These included the 2007 discovery of an unknown population of greater bamboo lemurs, *Prolemur simus*, which are critically endangered. They were found in a wetland habitat that was 240 miles (400km) from the only other group of the animals in the wild. Since 2000 the number of primate species has been boosted by the discovery of fifty-three previously unknown types: forty were from Madagascar, two from mainland Africa, and eight from Central and South America.

The red colobus is one of several primate species headed for extinction

Vanishing Jaguars

Camera traps placed in the Amazonian jungles are helping researchers to count how many jaguars remain in a region that is under pressure from oil exploration. Wildlife is under threat in two neighbouring protected areas in Ecuador because of the development that oil exploration brings in its wake. As more roads are built it becomes easier to gain access to once-remote areas of wilderness, and bushmeat hunters are able to move in.

The camera traps were placed in the Yasuni National Park and the Waorani Ethnic Reserve, which together encompass 500sq.miles (16,800 sq.km). Pictures taken by the camera traps show that jaguars are far less numerous in areas where they have to compete with humans for food. In the wilderness areas where significant bushmeat hunting was absent, the jaguars, the biggest cat in the Americas and the world's third biggest, were shown to be almost five times more common.

In one area of the Yasuni National Park, which is heavily hunted by people, only three jaguars were photographed. By contrast, fourteen different jaguars were recorded in a more remote area where there was little hunting by humans. Jaguars and other animals were photographed when their body heat, detected by special sensors, triggered the camera traps. Each of the jaguars could be identified because they have unique patterns of spots.

Scores of the big cats were pictured in the first two years of the project to count them in Ecuador, where conservationists regard them as vulnerable. The project was conducted by Santiago Espinosa of the University of Florida, Gainesville, in the US who selected four 25,000 acre zones to study –

> **Each of the jaguars could be identified because they have unique patterns of spots**

clockwise from opposite left: **Animals pictured by the camera traps include jaguars, short-eared dogs, two-toed sloths and white-lipped peccaries**

two of them in pristine Amazonian wilderness and two in areas where bushmeat hunting was common. His preliminary findings showed that where there is competition for food from human hunters in the forests there was less food available for the jaguars, with the result that the cats suffered a fall in numbers. Other animals recorded by the camera traps included a rarely-seen short-eared dog, a two-toed sloth mother and her baby, and several of the jaguar's prey species, such as white-lipped peccaries.

Camera traps were established as a reliable method of estimating big cat numbers when a study of tigers was carried out in India in the 1990s. Because each tiger's stripes are unique it was possible to establish how many individuals were in a region. The technique was adopted in Ecuador because the pattern of spots on jaguars are just as distinctive.

Conservation

A Place in the Ark

Knowledge is power just as much for conservationists trying to protect wildlife from the threat of extinction as it is for the most Machiavellian of politicians. As conservationists have attempted over the last hundred years or so to save species from being wiped out it has become increasingly clear that the first step toward preventing extinction is to understand the animal or plant involved. Detailed knowledge of diet, habits and preferred habitats greatly improves the chances of being able to provide the threatened species with the environment it needs to survive. Furthermore, it is increasingly recognised that conservation projects are more likely to meet with success if an entire habitat is protected rather than concentrating purely on a single species. By creating the right habitat it is not just the threatened species that benefits but a whole host of animals and plants.

Saving the Albatross

Sailors and naturalists alike have marvelled for centuries at the albatross's airborne mastery as it dips and soars over the ocean. The sight, however, has become increasingly rare as the birds have fallen victim to mankind's impact on their habits and habitats, and of the twenty-two species of albatross, nineteen are under threat of extinction.

Long-line fishing fleets pose one of the biggest threats to the birds. Conservationists estimate that up to 100,000 are killed by the boats annually – one every five minutes. The devastation caused to albatross populations prompted conservationists to launch an international campaign to persuade fishermen to change their techniques. The Albatross Task Force started work in 2006 and three years later it announced cuts of 85 per cent in the death toll in its first area of operations.

Long-line fishing presents a threat to albatrosses because it involves feeding baited hooks from the back of boats on lines that can stretch for miles. Unless the bait sinks quickly the birds can snatch it up, getting caught on the hooks and drowning. The impact of the deaths is made worse because while albatrosses have been known to live for more than half a century, they breed slowly and cannot raise chicks fast enough to make up for the damage caused by the long-line fishing industry. Albatrosses can be up to twelve years old before they breed and they produce only one chick at a time. Several species breed only in alternate years.

At the heart of the project was the determination to show fishermen, to whom every snagged bird was a waste of bait, that they could still earn a living from catching fish such as tuna, swordfish and Patagonian toothfish while protecting the birds. Equipment and fishing techniques exist which allow the fishermen to continue catching tuna and swordfish while ensuring that the bait disappears beneath the waves before albatrosses and other seabirds can fly in to seize any of the baited hooks. While teaching fishermen how to weight and feed their lines without catching albatrosses, the task force simultaneously lobbies governments to bring in legislation to protect seabirds, such as making it compulsory to report the number of birds killed on hooks each year.

The task force, a joint initiative between BirdLife International and the Royal Society for the Protection of Birds, began operating in South Africa. It succeeded in bringing about significant changes in fishing practices, which have led to 85 per cent fewer albatrosses being killed by South African fishing fleets. One of the most important factors in the success of the scheme was the willingness with which fishermen, despite initial suspicion among some, would listen to the conservationists. Instructors from the task force were even allowed to accompany fishing boats at sea to show where improvements could be made. In South Africa the task force succeeded in bringing in new regulations to limit the number of birds that each vessel can kill as accidental bycatch, and the introduction of a National Plan of Action to protect seabirds.

Preliminary results from other countries where the task force has begun campaigning suggest that the death toll has been reduced by as much as 67 per cent. Among the early improvements seen in Chilean waters, where death rates of albatrosses were even higher than anticipated, is a wide take-up of techniques to make bait sink faster and to scare birds away from the trailing lines. Similarly, forty per cent of the Brazilian long-line fishing fleets voluntarily adopted bird-friendly techniques ahead of mandatory measures. Other countries where the task force has begun operations include Namibia, Ecuador, Uruguay and Argentina. Three of the nineteen threatened species of albatross are down to such low levels that they are regarded as critically endangered: the Amsterdam, Chatham and Tristan albatrosses.

Chatham albatross, *Thalassarche eremita*, in flight

Humpback Recovery

Humpback whales have been taken off the endangered species list after bouncing back from the devastation wreaked by hunting in the 1960s. Damage to the humpback population, especially by the Soviet Union's Antarctic whaling fleet, drove the decision to introduce an international ban on hunting whales. Humpback numbers began rising in the 1980s and in 2008 they were, in a rare moment for conservationists, deemed high enough to be removed from the list of animals in danger of extinction.

Surveys of humpback whales, *Megaptera novaeangliae*, showed that at least 40,000 are now swimming the oceans. They are described by scientists at the International Union for the Conservation of Nature as among the species giving the "least concern" about their prospects. The whales, which can grow to more than 50ft (15m) long and weigh 40 tons, can live for 50 years, but females only give birth every two or three years and can be ten years old before they have their first calf. Calves can be more than 13ft (4m) long and two tons in weight when born.

Southern right whales, *Eubalaena australis*, are another species that have enjoyed a resurgence in recent years. Their numbers doubled to an estimated 15,000 in 2008, and were re-classified as of "least concern" having previously been considered "vulnerable to extinction". Similarly, Sei whales, *Balaenoptera borealis*, fin whales, *Balaenoptera physalus*, and blue whales, *Balaenoptera musculus*, are all rising in number.

Humpback whale calf above its mother, in the Pacific Ocean

This Little Piggy Came Home

A tiny pig that was once thought to be extinct has been reintroduced to the wild as part of a programme to ensure the species' long term survival. In 1964 Pygmy hogs were thought to have died out but hopes for their survival revived in 1971 when two small populations were found.

In 1995 conservationists from the Durrell Wildlife Conservation Trust captured six live animals in the wild and used them to found a captive breeding population for the Pygmy Hog Conservation Programme (PHCP). The animals bred successfully and in 2008 the first release took place as sixteen hogs – seven males and nine females – were set free in their natural grassland habitat in the Sonai Rupai wildlife sanctuary in Assam, India.

Follow-up surveys, which detected the presence of the pigs by locating the nests they build each day to sleep in, have shown that the animals are thriving in the wild. This conclusion is also supported by the pictures taken by static camera traps. Of the first 16 animals to be released, 12 to 14 are known to have survived their first year, and researchers discovered from footprints that one of the females had given birth, though the number of piglets was unclear. A second batch of pygmy hogs was released into Sonai Rupai in May 2009 and more reintroductions are likely to be carried out in the future. Captive pygmy hogs are kept in pre-release enclosures in Potasali, Assam, before they are released into the wild. The enclosures prepare them for freedom by replicating natural conditions while limiting the danger from predators and enabling scientists to monitor their progress.

Pygmy hogs, which are only 10-12in (25-30cm) tall and weigh just 6-9kg (13-20lb), are the smallest pigs in the world. Once the breeding programme began, scientists were able to observe the animals more closely than in the wild and realised that the species represented a previously unrecognised genus of pigs. According to Professor John Fa, of Durrell, this meant that they are as different from farmyard pigs, warthogs and boars as horses are from donkeys. In recognition of their new status the pygmy hogs were given a new Latin name, *Porcula salvanius*, to replace their old attribution, *Sus salvanius*.

The reintroduction programme was led by Durrell, which was founded by the naturalist and author Gerald Durrell, in partnership with Ecosystems India, the International Union for the Conservation of Nature, the regional government in Assam and the Indian government. Pygmy hogs were once common in the Indian sub-continent but a range of pressures, especially the loss of habitat to farmers, have shrunk their range.

Until the captive hogs were released the only place they were known to survive in the wild was

> Scientists realised that the species represented a previously unrecognised genus of pig

in the Manas National Park, in Assam, but the number still alive is thought to be as low as a thousand. Manas was discovered to be a last haven for the pigs in 1971 after four fresh corpses were found for sale on a market stall. A second population was also found at Barnardi in Assam, but has since died out. It was decided to reintroduce the captive animals at Sonai Rupai, – the species is thought to have once lived there – to reduce the risk of the pigs being wiped out in the event of a deadly disease or another catastrophe at Manas.

The existing population at Manas is already under severe pressure because of farming practices. The hogs depend on grassland for shelter and food but research has revealed that the entire habitat is deliberately burnt at least once a year. The hog population can sustain the losses to predators and even the limited poaching that goes on but the fires threaten to further reduce their numbers.

Pygmy hogs mainly eat succulents and tubers but also consume lizards, insects, and small rodents when given the opportunity. Their body shape is designed to make it easier for them to push their way through thick grasses, and they make nests during the hottest part of the day by scraping a hollow into the ground and pushing soft vegetation into it. Data gathered from the monitoring of released hogs is helping scientists build up a better picture of how the species acts in the wild. In the long run this information should help researchers work out how best to protect the hogs in the Manas National Park.

above: *Porcula salvanius*, the pygmy pig

Bat's off the Menu

A fruit bat, which was prized as a delicacy by islanders has been brought back from the brink of extinction. The Pemba flying fox, *Pteropus voeltzkowi*, was found to be in dire straits when fewer than ten were spotted in 1989. Three years later the total numbers were estimated at 2,400 to 3,600, and although this was better than feared, the numbers had declined dramatically compared to a decade earlier.

The species is found only on the island of Pemba off the east coast of Africa where it used to be hunted for the pot and was regarded as especially delicious if roasted. In recent decades 95 per cent of the island's forests have been cut down resulting in habitat loss that has had a serious impact on Pemba flying fox numbers, and this damage has been exacerbated by hunting. The problem became even more acute with the introduction of shotguns, which made it much easier to kill the bats than the traditional method of catching them in traps on long sticks.

However, numbers today have increased dramatically after a conservation programme was started in the 1990s to protect the bat. The project, by Fauna & Flora International in partnership with Tanzania's Department of Commercial Crops, Fruit and Forestry, proved successful and by 2009 it was calculated that the flying fox population had increased to at least 22,000 and perhaps even to 35,600. Villagers were persuaded that rather than regarding the bat as something to eat, they should value it for other reasons such as the potential to attract eco-tourists and its importance in pollinating plants and distributing seeds around the island. It is thought to be of particular importance to the plants with the largest seeds because it is probably the only species on the island that can distribute them.

Pemba flying foxes, which have distinctive chestnut-orange fur, feed on fruit such as figs, breadfruit and mangos, and on leaves and flowers. Seeds are dispersed in droppings. People on the island have rallied enthusiastically to the cause of the flying fox, and many villagers have established environmental clubs to help protect nearby roosts. Some roosts now contain more than a thousand bats. The species has a wingspan of 5.5ft (1.7m) – wider than the average woman is tall – and weighs about 0.9-1.4lbs (0.4-0.65kg).

> The species is found only on the island of Pemba, where it was hunted for the pot

The Butterfly Back from the Dead

A butterfly's salvation has become a blueprint for recovery and reintroduction after the insect became extinct in the UK and suffered severe losses in other parts of Europe. The large blue butterfly, *Maculinea arion*, died out in the UK in 1979 despite being the focus of conservation work for decades, but it is now back in its thousands. Butterfly collectors were originally blamed for the extinction but they were exonerated when research revealed that changes in the way grasslands were grazed was the true culprit.

Professor Jeremy Thomas of the University of Oxford and the Centre for Ecology and Hydrology in the UK has spent more than thirty years studying the butterfly and was instrumental in its recovery. He was already involved in efforts to save the large blue when the last of the British population disappeared in 1979. Efforts to help the insect included sitting in fields observing any detail that might be relevant to its survival, including counting all the eggs and observing the caterpillars' movements. He described his work as the "insect equivalent to living with the apes" and it yielded vital information when he realised the importance to the butterfly of a tiny ant and the height of grass. Ecologists were aware that the large blue used ants to protect its caterpillars, but only when the creatures came under the scrutiny of Professor Thomas did the ecologists realise the level of dependence of the butterflies on a single species of ant.

The caterpillars are taken into the nests of several species of ants but it is only those picked up by *Myrmica sabuleti* that have a reasonable chance of making it to adulthood. Large blue caterpillars hatch on thyme plants and drop to the ground where the ants are tricked by chemical secretions into treating them as ant larvae. Once they have taken the caterpillars to their nests the ants continue to protect them, seemingly unaware that the caterpillars are eating the ant grubs.

Professor Thomas and his colleagues further realised that *M. sabuleti* was in rapid decline, and by analysing all the possible factors involved they worked out that changes in the way grasslands were being maintained was killing off the ant. Grazing livestock had been moved off the grassland sites where the ants lived, which meant the vegetation became overgrown. Simultaneously, rabbit numbers were at an historically low ebb. As the vegetation grew, the soil temperature fell to the point that it was too cool for the ants, and as they disappeared, so did the butterflies.

Once the full extent of the mutual dependencies was recognised it became possible for conservationists planning a reintroduction to ensure that the butterflies and the ants were provided with ideal habitats by clearing scrub and bringing back grazing animals. They also realised that some previous attempts to protect the large blue had been counterproductive, including the erection of a fence around a colony in 1931 to deter collectors. It also kept out grazing animals and the large blue population quickly vanished.

The first reintroductions, using butterflies from Sweden, took place in 1983, and by 2008 the project had been so successful that there were 30 per cent more large blue butterfly colonies in the UK than there had been in 1950.

Some of the new colonies have now reached saturation point and the butterflies have steadily increased their range since 1983. Large blues have returned in such numbers that colonies can boast 4,000 to 5,000 individuals, and they have spread naturally from their reintroduction sites to at least twenty-five locations.

The discoveries made by Professor Thomas and his colleagues have helped guide the conservation of several types of butterfly in Europe and other parts of the world, by showing, for example, that the specific needs of the young can drive a species' survival. The researchers involved in the study of the large blue's needs said that the problems facing the insect, and the type of information needed to solve them, were typical of many temperate butterflies.

opposite: **The large blue butterfly, *Maculinea arion***
below: **Ecologists realised that the ants were in rapid decline**

Genetic Fingerprinting for Buffalos

Animals on the verge of extinction are being given a lifeline by technology more commonly used to identify criminals. Individual animals are being singled out from the herd by the use of genetic fingerprinting, which has been used by police forces around the world since the 1980s. Cutting edge CSI-style genetic tests have been taken up by researchers who are using them to gain crucial insights into the lifestyles of two species of dwarf buffalo and the numbers that are left.

Scientists trying to save the buffalo, the Tamaraw in the Philippines and the Anoa in Indonesia, have resorted to genetics because other methods of studying them, such as tracking, have failed. Understanding the habits and requirements of the two forest-dwelling species, such as how far they roam in search of food, will help researchers identify the best means of protecting the animals, which are related to the two-ton water buffalo found on the Asian mainland.

To get genetic samples for analysis the researchers resorted to collecting more than 150 'buffalo pats', the semi-liquid faeces, which contained fragments of DNA from the stomach lining. From this material the research team from the University of Hull in the UK have gleaned details of the animals that could not be ascertained previously, including ages, relationships, state of health, and geographic spread.

Only 3,000 Anoas are thought to remain and they are found only on the Indonesian island of Sulawesei, where the biggest threats to their existence are the destruction of the forests they live in and hunting by indigenous people. Conservationists estimate that fewer than 500 Tamaraw, the largest land animals in the Philippines, survive on the island of Mindoro. Most of their natural forest habitat has been cut down, largely to make way for agriculture, and they are today confined to between six and seven per cent of their historic territory, though the authorities have in recent years afforded them some legal protection. Both of the dwarf buffalos have horns that face backwards. Were they to have forward-facing horns they would forever be getting snagged on creepers and branches. Anoa and Tamaraw are both much smaller than their mainland cousin, with whom they shared a common ancestor three million years ago, but at a quarter to a third of a ton each they are still an intimidating sight for any researcher who gets too close.

> Cutting edge CSI-style genetic tests can give crucial insights into the dwarf buffalo

Details that have been uncovered by the genetic research into their lifestyles include the size of breeding populations and how far each animal roams. Interactions between each animal, especially over mating rights, are being closely studied as part of attempts to establish how many fertile males and females survive. One type of behaviour the CSI-style tests can shed light on is whether the Tamaraw have, as suspected, jealously-guarded harems. Once the genes have yielded enough clues about the animals' lifestyles and patterns of behaviour, conservationists will be able to decide how best to help them, such as by giving special protection to the parts of the forest that are most important to them.

Their success in pinpointing signature genes – marker genes – that reveal the species' identity has made it possible to distinguish the animals from feral livestock, an important step if the wild buffalo are to be conserved without their DNA being diluted by domesticated strains. Analysis of mitochondrial DNA, which is inherited through the female line, has made it possible for researchers, led by Dr Philip Wheeler and Dr Bill Hutchinson, to identify families of buffalo. Much less nuclear DNA than mitochondrial DNA – a thousand times less – is contained in the pats, but when it is found it offers much more information about an individual. By fine-tuning their techniques researchers have begun the task of using it to identify every one of the animals still alive.

The researchers believe that these genetic techniques should prove equally useful when applied to other rare, little-understood creatures that need protecting from extinction. These include the Congo forest buffalo, the European bison in Poland, the okapi in Central Africa, Baird's tapir in Honduras, and the saola of Vietnam, which was discovered in 1992.

Genetic fingerprinting is helping researchers study the lowland anoa

Whale Breath

Whale breath has been collected as part of a project to ascertain how healthy the cetaceans are and what diseases they suffer from. Remote controlled model helicopters were used to take samples as whales came to the surface to expel old breath and to replenish it with fresh oxygen-rich supplies. Samples from the spouts were taken by fitting the machines with sterilised Petri dishes and flying them directly into the clouds of gas, water and mucus exhaled from the whales' blowholes.

The project, an initiative by the Zoological Society of London (ZSL) in collaboration with the National Polytechnic University of Mexico, aims to identify the pathogens that affect whales. Analysis of whale diseases has previously concentrated on primarily sick, stranded or dead animals because they are much easier to reach than healthy animals, but such sampling is not considered representative of the normal population.

The technique of flying helicopters through exhaled whale breath was devised to enable researchers to get close enough to take samples from live whales in their natural habitat without harming them. For some whales, especially grey whales, it was possible for scientists in research vessels to get close enough to the surfacing animals to get a sample of breath by leaning out with a Petri dish on the end of a long pole. But in most cases the whales kept their distance and researchers had to come up with another way of getting to the exhaling whales in time to take a sample. Sperm whales and blue whales in particular tend to stay clear of boats.

Remote controlled model helicopters were used to sample the breath

The helicopter technique was invented by Dr Karina Acevedo-Whitehouse of ZSL who hopes that enough samples will eventually be gathered and analysed to provide the first global assessment of the health of the whale population. In the course of studying whales, Dr Acevedo-Whitehouse has managed to get close enough to some of the animals to get splattered by the water and mucus in their spouts and to smell their breath herself. In many cases the breath smelt, predictably enough she said, of the ocean but in some cases the smell was so foul that it seemed likely the animal was sick. Once the Petri dishes have been removed from the model aircraft the pathogens can be identified by analysing the DNA traces left by the whale breath.

Most of the testing was carried out in the Gulf of California off the coast of Mexico and was also conducted on a smaller scale off Gibraltar. The species sampled included blue, pilot and grey whales, and bottle-nosed dolphins. Model helicopters were chosen over model aeroplanes because they can be kept hovering close to a spot where a whale is expected to surface. Once researchers have succeeded in spotting a pod of whales or an individual animal they can often predict where the animals will next rise to the surface.

Whale spouts vary in height and duration from species to species. Sperm whales can hold their breath for more than forty minutes and tend to blow out for longer than other species, whereas blue whales blow out used air in several short bursts lasting for only about a second each.

The blue whale, *Baelenoptra musculus* blowing a spout of gas, water and mucus from its blowhole

Images of Hope

Pictures of critically endangered Javan rhinos splashing in muddy pools have provided renewed hope for the survival of the species. Javan rhinos, *Rhinoceros sondaicus*, are among the most endangered animals in the world with just sixty thought to be left in the wild. Efforts to conserve them are hampered because scientists know so little about their behaviour, needs and preferences in their natural habitat. They can weigh more than two tons and reach 11.5ft (4m) long yet they are rarely seen because they avoid humans – although they will attack if anyone gets too close.

A network of 34 camera traps placed in the the Ujung Kulon National Park in Java as part of a conservation programme involving several organisations, including WWF, has given researchers a window on the elusive animal. Several images taken by the cameras, which provide researchers with a mixture of stills and video footage, have shown the animals wallowing in muddy pools. Another showed a female chasing off a wild pig from a mud hole. Conservationists viewing the pictures have also gained insights into the rhino's nocturnal activities because some of the cameras have an infra-red facility.

On Java, where the animals were once numerous, there is thought to be a population of about fifty. It is the only known population of the rhinos that has had any success in breeding in recent years. At the Cat Tien National Park in Vietnam there are known to be ten Javan rhinos but none appear to have given birth for several years and conservationists fear that they are incapable of breeding.

> Javan rhinos are among the most endangered animals in the world

Conservationists are hoping to be able to identify a second area on Java where the animals can live. The images from the cameras should assist them with the selection as they can identify the plants the animals need. The Indonesian government has backed the research. According to Susie Ellis of the International Rhino Foundation the relocation of some of the rhinos will reduce the chances of all the rhinos being wiped out by a single catastrophe, such as disease or volcanic eruption.

Camera traps in Liberia have proved similarly useful in revealing that pygmy hippos are still occupying the Sapa National Park despite the country being wracked by civil wars from 1989 to 1996 and 1999 to 2003. The pygmy hippo is a secretive animal and is extremely difficult to spot, but camera traps had photographed it within three days of being set up by researchers from the Zoological Society of London, Fauna & Flora International and the Forestry Development Agency in Liberia.

Estimates have put the population of pygmy hippos in the wild at about 3,000, although this figure is considered unreliable because so little research has been carried out. Conservationists are anxious to get a clearer idea of the threat posed to the endangered species and the camera traps are helping to monitor the surviving population. The Upper Guinean forest where the pygmy hippos, *Hexaprotodon liberiensis*, live has been mostly destroyed and just 10 per cent of it is left; 40 per cent of the remainder is in Liberia. The animal is also found in Ivory Coast and Sierra Leone.

The Indian rhino is a close cousin of the Javan rhino, and shares many of its unusual features, including a single horn and heavily folded skin

Frog Rescue

Some of the last survivors of a species of frog have been airlifted to safety after a deadly disease threatened to drive them into extinction. Tens of thousands of mountain chicken frogs were estimated to live on the Caribbean island of Montserrat in 2008, but when the deadly chytrid fungal disease reached the island in January 2009 they died in droves.

Conservationists, recognising the urgency of the problem, launched an emergency rescue operation to catch enough frogs to form a captive breeding population before it was too late. Researchers managed to track down fifty of the mountain chicken frogs on Montserrat and airlifted them into captivity. They were split between the Zoological Society of London, the Durrell Wildlife Conservation Trust in Jersey, and Parken Zoo in Sweden. Within six months of the fungal disease reaching the island just a few hundred frogs were thought to have survived. Most of the survivors were in a valley so remote that the disease had not reached it, but a few others clung on in a second part of the island about a two-hour walk away.

Chytridiomycosis had reached the second location and was ravaging the frogs in the area, but in an innovative attempt at saving the species scientists have started treating the animals in the wild with an anti-fungal treatment that had proved successful on captive amphibians. Scientists are monitoring the treatment scheme closely because it offers hope of saving at least a small number of frogs around the world from the chytrid fungus.

The fungus has been spreading rapidly around the world and has taken a devastating toll of many species. The fungal infection is the single biggest threat to amphibians and some scientists estimate that, along with other factors such as loss of habitat, it could result in a third of all the world's 6,000 amphibian species being driven into extinction.

Mountain chicken frogs, *Leptodactylus falla*, were once common on several Caribbean islands, where they were regarded as a nutritious delicacy. They had died out on most of the islands – one of the biggest factors in their disappearance was the introduction of the mongoose – but had survived on Montserrat and Dominica. On Dominica, where they are included in the island's coat of arms, they were eaten widely until numbers slumped because of the arrival of the fungus.

The 2009 emergency rescue operation on Montserrat was the second time that conservationists had to act quickly to help the species. Chytrid reached Dominica in 2002 and by 2004 most of the frogs had vanished. In 2007 researchers set out to remove as many of the survivors as possible and keep them in protective custody in captivity. Only six of the frogs could be found on Dominica and with just three males heard calling in 2009 the species is regarded as "ecologically extinct" on the island, said Dr Andrew Cunningham of ZSL, one of the senior scientists involved in the rescues. Montserrat was the frog's last stronghold so when the disease was detected on the island – probably introduced by a tree frog imported accidentally on produce – conservationists knew they had to act fast to prevent them vanishing all together.

The captive populations will be used to keep the species alive even if it is wiped out in the wild, and could be used as the basis for a re-introduction programme in the future. Mountain chicken frogs are among the biggest frogs in the world and can weigh more than 2lbs (0.9kg).

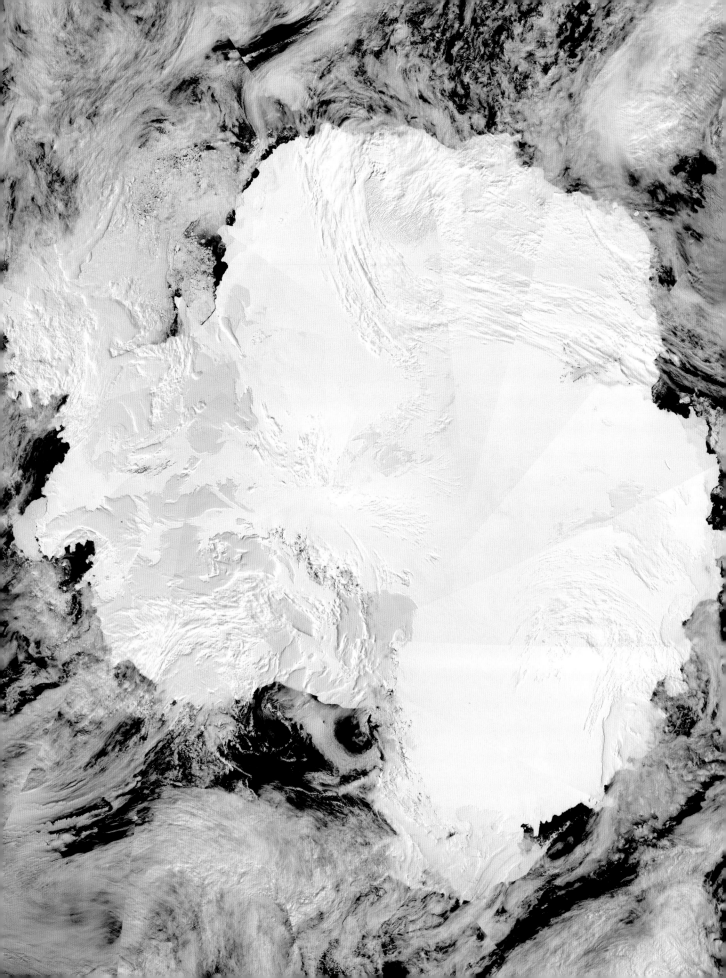

Poo Prints

Satellite imaging has helped to pinpoint the locations of emperor penguin breeding colonies on the sea ice in Antarctica. The breeding colonies are difficult to spot by conventional methods because of the severe weather encountered during winter and the distances involved. But because the penguins leave a distinctive reddish-brown stain on the ice and snow with their guano, pictures taken from space have been able to reveal their whereabouts.

Scientists with the British Antarctic Survey (BAS) used the images to find 38 emperor breeding colonies. Of these, ten were previously unknown and six were from colonies that had relocated. There was no sign, however, of the six colonies that were known to researchers, and their loss has deepened concerns about a decline in emperor penguin numbers.

The use of satellite images should help conservation of the aquatic birds by providing data on their whereabouts and their responses to environmental changes. Individual penguins cannot be seen in the images that were taken of the sea ice around 90 per cent of the Antarctic coast, but because the males spend eight months on the ice their guano is readily visible.

Once female emperor penguins have laid their eggs they return to sea until the spring, leaving the males on the sea ice to endure temperatures of minus 50°C or more. Once the eggs hatch in spring the females return to allow the males to go back to the water to feed.

opposite: **Satellite images of Antarctica**
above right: **Penguin guano is readily visible on ice**
below: **Emperor penguins**

Deforested Haven

Tropical forest feared to be virtually worthless for conservation purposes has been found to harbour unexpectedly rich levels of wildlife. A survey in Sumatra has shown that wild animals continue to use forest habitats even when they have been badly degraded by logging and agricultural developments. Tigers, clouded leopards and elephants were among the species that used the damaged forests as a haven. The survey findings suggested that even areas of secondary forest that had suffered severe damage could be worth preserving for their conservation value to rare animals.

Evidence for the high levels of animal use in degraded forest was provided by a series of camera traps laid out in a 772 sq.mile (2,000 sq.km) area on the Indonesian island, backed up by sightings of animals and their footprints. Pictures taken when an animal triggered the cameras revealed the presence of 38 species of medium to large creatures, 18 of which are classified as threatened. Five different tigers, each distinguishable by the variations in their striped markings, dhole and tapirs were among the camera trap discoveries that most surprised the researchers in the forest remnants. Other animals included leopard cats, the short-tailed mongoose, and banded linsangs.

It was the first time that researchers were able to provide "concrete proof", said Sarah Christie of the Zoological Society of London (ZSL), of the value of degraded areas to wildlife. Previously it was assumed that many of the mammals had abandoned the territory once it was disturbed by logging and other destructive activities, yet they were found in sustainable numbers.

> **Many species continued to use the damaged forests as a haven**

The study area was a mix of palm oil cropland, scrubland and degraded forest in the Jambi province and the survey was carried out by researchers from ZSL, the Frankfurt Zoological Society in Germany, the Indonesian Forestry Department (PHKA) and Bukit 30 National Park.

As well as highlighting the value of damaged forests for many animals, the survey also revealed that few mammals will remain on land planted with palm oil crops. Only common mammals, including leopard cats, bearded pigs and the common palm civet were recorded regularly on the palm oil plantations, whereas those considered rare – notably Sumatran tigers, dhole, clouded leopards and tapirs – avoided the crop.

opposite and below: **Logging roads in Indonesia** overleaf: **Clouded leopards were found to still inhabit deforested areas**

A Confusion of Identities

A sponge found to have more than four dozen different guises in scientific literature has had to have its habitat range reassessed. The breadcrumb sponge, *Halichondria panicea*, has managed to be "discovered" and named on 56 different occasions since first being described in 1766. It comes in so many colours, shapes and sizes that over the last two and a half centuries naturalists repeatedly made the mistake of thinking they had discovered a new species. Names attributed to the sponge, which smells of gunpowder, included *Alcyonium manusdiaboli* in 1794, *Spongia compacta* in 1806 and *Trachyopsilla glaberrima* in 1931.

It was just one of thousands of animals and plants living in the seas that were found to have multiple identities during the compilation of a comprehensive catalogue of marine life. More than 56,000 species names, almost a third of the known total, have now had to be erased from the roll call of life in the seas. The breadcrumb sponge was the most extreme example, but there were plenty more creatures that had been named at least twice. Among them were a type of sea squirt, *Cnemidocarpa verrucosa*, which boasted nineteen Latin names and the spiny dogfish, *Squalus acanthias*, with twenty-one different identities. Even supposedly well-known animals, such as the basking shark, managed to confuse researchers with multiple identities after being given forty different names.

The modern system of identifying animals and plants with Latin names was devised by Carl Linnaeus, a Swedish botanist regarded as the Father of Taxonomy. He had wanted to reduce the confusion caused when species found in a variety of places around the world went under different names. Common whelks in Britain were known as bulots in France and biccins in Canada but once provided with the Latin name *Buccinum undatum* the creature was recognised as the same wherever it was found. Linnaeus, for all the brilliance of his system, was guilty himself of providing at least one animal with multiple identities. He treated the sperm whale as four different species, and although the mistake has long been recognised, the tags still crop up in some databases and the literature.

There are several reasons why thousands of species received more than one name, simple misspelling being one of them. Over-eagerness for the glory of discovering an animal or plant new to science and a corresponding reluctance to make sufficient checks was also attributed as a factor, as were mistaken interpretations of features when describing a species.

The 56,396 unjustified names were identified by scientists working on the Census for Marine Life (CoML). They made up 32 per cent of the 178,995 names of marine creatures and plants recorded as living in the seas by early 2008 and assessed by the census team. Once the multiple identities were discounted there were 122,559 species regarded as verified but the number is expected to rise dramatically as the census project continues. It is estimated that more than 230,000 marine species have been recorded overall and that more than a million will eventually be found and recognised.

The basking shark was given forty different names

Pick out a Penguin

Trying to pick out an individual penguin from a crowd of thousands is a daunting task for the keenest of eyes but researchers now have technology to help them. A recognition system has been created to distinguish each of the 20,000 jackass penguins found on South Africa's Robben Island. Instead of looking at the faces of the animals, the system concentrates on the animals' chests and stomachs, which have patterns of black spots on a white background. The most common number of spots is twelve, but jackass penguins, *Spheniscus demersus*, more properly known as African penguins, can have as many as twenty or as few as two. The black spots are usually formed of just three or four feathers but that is enough for the computerised recognition system.

Recognising individual penguins is useful to researchers because it allows them to follow the movement patterns of single animals within huge colonies. African penguins known as jackasses because they make a call that sounds like a braying donkey, are in decline, and by finding out more about their habits conservationists hope to identify ways of helping them. By tracking individuals researchers are able to learn much more about the animals, such as their average lifespan, how long each one stays at sea, how they are affected by factors such as fish stock movements and changes to the climate, and how often they need to feed. Tagging the penguins could provide much of the information but their sharp beaks and willingness to fight any scientist who has the temerity to try to grab them make such an

A special camera records the spot patterns of all the penguins that waddle past it

approach a stressful affair for all involved. The recognition system allows researchers to follow the penguins without having to get too close to them. Details of each bird's features are logged by a special camera, which records the spot patterns of all the penguins that waddle past it. It was set up on a path that penguins took to reach the water to feed, and the system managed to identify 20 per cent of the animals on the island in a day, and 98 per cent of them in a month.

Professor Peter Barham of the University of Bristol in the UK led the research that created the system, with the support of Earthwatch and the Leverhulme Trust. As a professor of physics he specialises in studying the properties of polymers but he has become involved in conservation because he is fanatical about penguins. The system was created by a collaboration between the University of Bristol and the University of Cape Town in South Africa. It was originally designed to identify penguin spots but has the potential to monitor a range of different animals, such as whales and butterflies.

An estimated two million African penguins were found on the southern African coast a century ago but now it is feared that there are fewer than 200,000 breeding birds left. They were badly hit by egg hunting and the removal of the guano into which they dug their nests in the twentieth century. In the last decade it is feared the penguins have suffered from the impact of climate change, which is suspected of driving sardines and anchovies away from the birds' feeding grounds.

Rediscovered Species

Wildlife, Lost and Found

S ome of the secrets uncovered by scientists studying the natural world are as much re-discoveries as they are new findings. Perhaps the most famous of these was the coelacanth, a fish that was known from the fossil record but was presumed to have become extinct about 65 million years ago. In 1938, to the astonishment of scientists and the public alike, one was caught off the east coast of South Africa. Other animals are still being rediscovered today and though they may be less spectacular finds than the coelacanth they are still a source of fascination, and in many cases relief. Rediscoveries can be made in museums where specimens are overlooked for decades before their significance is noticed or realised. Equally, they can be made in the field where evidence of creatures thought long dead can be uncovered.

Party Bird

The critically endangered sociable lapwing was thought to be on the verge of extinction until more than a thousand of the birds were spotted in a single day. The species was regarded as one of the world's rarest and most threatened birds, and estimates had put its population as low as 400 individuals.

In early 2007, however, ornithologists monitoring a grassland site popular with birds stopping off in northern Syria on migration were astounded to see 1,200 sociable lapwings in a day. The Syrian Sociable Lapwing Team, a group of Syrian and Dutch birdwatchers, continued to watch the area and recorded a total of 1,500 sociable lapwings. Remco Hofland, the Dutch ornithologist who led the team, described the find as a dream come true.

Another nearby bird feeding site, across the Turkish border, was thought to be a further possible location for sociable lapwings, so two watchers set out to see if any had turned up. On their second day at Ceylanpinar, about 15 miles (25km) from the Syrian sightings, they recorded 1,017 of the birds. A few months later an even bigger population of sociable lapwings, *Vanellus gregarious*, was located at the Ceylanpinar feeding ground in south-eastern Turkey as scientists followed the progress of a bird fitted with a satellite tracker on its migration to Africa for the winter.

Dr Rob Sheldon, of the Royal Society for the Protection of Birds (RSPB) had tagged the lapwing in Kazakhstan before it flew 2,000 miles (3,220km) to Turkey. When signals showed that it had stopped in Ceylanpinar watchers decided to take a closer look and spotted 1,800 of the birds. The following day they saw even more – 3,200.

The birds in Ceylanpinar were counted and observed by researchers from Doga Dernegi (Birdlife in Turkey) who described the discovery of the flock as hugely significant for the conservation of the species. Guven Eken, the director, commented that the sociable lapwings were finally living up to their name.

Sociable lapwings were once widespread in Central Asia and Russia but suffered a population crash in the twentieth century. From 1930 to 1960 numbers fell by 40 per cent and there was a further 50 per cent loss from 1960 to 1987. One suspected cause of this is the transformation of parts of the Steppes into agricultural land during the era of the Soviet Union, as well as hunting in the Middle East. Despite this, researchers remain unclear as to why so many of the birds should have been lost, although hunting is regarded as one of the biggest continuing threats.

Sociable lapwings are so named because the birds used to be found in huge flocks, and the sound of many hundreds or thousands of the birds calling to each other sounded as though they were chattering amongst themselves.

> **Ornithologists were astonished to see 1,200 sociable lapwings in a day**

A sociable lapwing stretching its wings

Done Rare

Evidence of an endangered animal's continued existence has been provided by a hunter who caught one – and promptly ate it. "It was delicious," said the tribesman who was unaware that the creature, Attenborough's long-beaked echidna, was assumed to be extinct.

The animal, an egg-laying mammal related to the platypus, lives in Papua New Guinea and is so rare that it has been seen only once by scientists. A specimen was collected in 1961 but it was only in 1998 that researchers realised it represented an unknown species, by which time they had decided it was almost certainly extinct.

In 2007, however, members of an expedition to Papua New Guinea's Cyclops Mountains spoke to villagers who called it a payangko and insisted that they had seen it. The most recent sighting was in 2005 by the hunter who caught one in a snare, and four other hunters gave convincing accounts of capturing them. A less well corroborated report was provided by a sixth hunter who said he had seen one in early 2007.

Despite the report of the echidnas being eaten the researchers were encouraged because it meant the creatures were still to be found. Moreover, they found several holes – known as nose pokes – in termite mounds or in the ground, into which the echidna had thrust its distinctive long beak in search of termites or worms to eat. In some places the animals had pushed their noses into the soft ground so firmly that there were impressions of their heads in the mud. Burrows were also located but none w occupied.

Attenborough's long-beaked echidna, *Zaglossus attenboroughi*, is the smallest of the four types of echidna, three of which are long-beaked and one short-beaked. All three long-beaked echidnas live on Papua New Guinea; the short-beaked species is found in Australia and New Guinea. Along with the platypus they are the only living egg-laying mammals, known as monotremes.

The expedition to find evidence of the echidna's survival was led by Dr Jonathan Baillie as part of the Zoological Society of London's Edge Programme, which focuses on the conservation and study of some of the world's most threatened animals. Accounts by villagers, who were clearly familiar with the echidna, and the nose pokes discovered by the researchers established that the animal can live at much lower levels in the mountains than previously thought. The original specimen was found at 5,250ft (1,600m) near the peak of Mount Rara, but more recent evidence has shown that its habitat can be as low as 525ft (160m).

It was clear from conversations with villagers in the Cyclops Mountains that echidnas have a part in their culture. Wrong-doers in the small town of Wambena can be punished by being forced to either pay a fine or find one of the animals. In another town, Dormena, it is said that conflicts between two opposing families or groups of people can be brought to an end by eating an echidna together.

Attenborough's long-beaked echidna was recognised as a separate species in 1998 by Professor Tim Flannery, director of the South Australia Museum, and Professor Colin Groves of the Australian National University. They reached their conclusion after analysing the specimen from the National Museum of Natural History in the Netherlands, which had been found in Papua New Guinea in 1961. It is the only specimen known to exist of the species and it was named after Sir David Attenborough, the UK broadcaster and naturalist.

Alive and Breeding

Evidence has been found of a healthy breeding colony of a seabird which ornithologists thought had been extinct for almost 78 years. Beck's petrel was found around an archipelago in the Pacific Ocean close to where it had originally been discovered in 1928. More than thirty of the petrels were photographed including many recently fledged juveniles, indicating the presence of at least one breeding colony.

It was found by Hadoram Shirihai, a leading ornithologist and an expert on bird identification, who was convinced he had seen the species in 2003 but lacked independent evidence to convince others. He was so determined to find the petrel that in 2007 he hired a boat to take him around the islands of the Bismarck Archipelago, part of Papua New Guinea. Beck's petrels appeared on seven of the expedition's thirteen days, and on one occasion Mr Shirihai was able to scoop the body of a newly dead fledgling from the sea. Its body, only the third specimen of Beck's petrel ever to be collected, provided cast iron proof of the bird's continuing existence.

Until Mr Shirihai spotted and photographed Beck's petrels, *Pseudobulweria becki*, there had only been a handful of unconfirmed sightings since 1929. Without photographic evidence of the bird's survival to back up sightings, reports were treated with caution by bird authorities because of its similarity and easy confusion with the Tahiti petrel, *P. Rostrata*.

Beck's petrel was discovered in 1928 by Rollo Beck, who, as one of the leading ornithologists of the early twentieth century, was commissioned by the American Museum of Natural History to collect and discover specimens for study. He collected his first Beck's petrel, which was later named after him, in 1928, and his second in 1929, which was the last time the bird was known to be alive until it was rediscovered by Mr Shirihai.

The method used by Mr Shirihai to attract the petrels close enough to observe and photograph them is called chumming and appropriately, was originally developed by Mr Beck. It involves placing frozen blocks of fish and fish oil in the sea for the birds to use as floating feeding stations.

A juvenile Beck's petrel, photographed by Hadoram Shirihai during the expedition to the Bismarck archipelago when the species was rediscovered to science

Time Capsule Seed

An extinct date palm has been brought back from the dead after a 2,000-year-old seed was dug up and germinated. The seed is the oldest ever known to germinate successfully and was recovered from excavations of Masada, a fortress overlooking the Dead Sea that was built by King Herod in the first century BC.

The plant that sprouted from the seed is thought to be a Judean date palm, a type that has since disappeared but once flourished in the Jordan River valley. Archaeologists found several seeds underneath rubble in the 1960s, and once they were dug up they remained in storage at room temperature until three were given to Dr Sarah Sallon, director of the Louis Borick Natural Medicine Research Centre at Hadassah University Hospital in Israel. She decided it was worth seeing if the seeds would still germinate so she passed one to Dr Elaine Solowey of the Arava Institute for Environmental Studies in Israel to plant after soaking it in water and fertilisers. To their delight the seed germinated and the seedling was named Methuselah after the oldest person mentioned in the Old Testament. Methuselah was reputed to have lived to the age of 969.

Small pieces were chipped off the other two seeds and sent to Dr Markus Egli of the University of Zurich in Switzerland for radiocarbon dating, which pinpointed their age as about 2,000 years, most likely from the first century BC or the first century AD. Further radiocarbon dating was carried out on the germinated seed when it was re-potted at the age of fifteen months. Fragments of the seed shell were found clinging to the roots and they were sent to Zurich where it was confirmed that they were about 2,000 years old. Prior to Methuselah, which by mid-2009 was more than 6.5ft (2m) tall, the oldest seed to be germinated was a 1,300-year-old lotus seed from China.

The Judean date palm that grew from a 2,000-year-old seed

Judean date palms were common in parts of the Middle East 2,000 years ago have but have now disappeared. It is thought that the hot, dry conditions in the Dead Sea region helped preserve the seed. Dates grown in Israel today derive from other strains, but the successful germination of the seedling has raised hopes that the Judean variety can be revived. Work is under way to try to revive more seeds of a similar age.

Preliminary analysis of Methuselah shows that it shares approximately half its genes with modern varieties of dates, including the Moroccan Medjool, Egypt's Hayani, and the Iraqi Barhee cultivars. In the first century AD Judean dates were renowned for their sweet taste and medicinal qualities and were grown extensively in the Dead Sea region. Pliny the Elder was among those who admired their taste and succulence, and the description he gave suggested that at 2-3in (5-8cm) long they were especially big for dates. Historical documents show that the date palm was considered particularly valuable for the treatment of lung diseases, including tuberculosis, and cancer.

The fortress where the seeds were found was used by King Herod as a palace and was built on a high point overlooking the Dead Sea. During the Revolt of the Jews in the first century AD it was used as a base by the rebels to harass Roman forces until it was besieged. When it became clear to those defending it in 74AD that they were about to be overrun by the Romans, they are reputed to have committed mass suicide.

It is uncertain exactly when widespread cultivation of the date palm ended, but it is likely to have been in sharp decline by the end of the second century AD. Any meaningful cultivation had probably ended by the tenth century, and when nineteenth century naturalists recorded plants in the region they could find only a few straggly date palms growing wild.

Cold cases

Just as detectives are able to make arrests by revisiting old cases so researchers are able to discover unknown types of animals in museum archives. Insects are the creatures most commonly discovered in the vaults but larger animals have also turned up.

A previously unrecognised bird from Colombia was discovered in the Natural History Museum in the United Kingdom during research for a comprehensive guide, the *Handbook of the Birds of the World*. The Antioquia brown-banded antpitta, *Grallaria milleri gilesi*, was realised to be new to science when discrepancies were noted between the description of the Yellow-breasted antpitta for the new book and the drawing that had been done of a museum specimen by Norman Arlott. It was realised that the specimen that had been put in the archives had been mis-recorded and should have been put down as a brown-banded antpitta.

Further close inspection, however, revealed that there were differences between the specimen and other brown-banded antpittas, such as leg length. Dr Robert Prys-Jones and Dr Paul Salaman of the museum realised that they had a new type of antpitta on their hands and described it as a sub-species of the brown-banded variety. They were confident that it justified being regarded as a full species, except that with only one specimen available it was impossible to be certain. Attempts to extract DNA from the preserved bird's toe pads proved unsuccessful. Attempts were made to find live examples in the wild but after intensive searches by Fundación ProAves, the national bird conservation organisation in Colombia, it was concluded that the bird had died out since the specimen was collected.

The single thrush-sized specimen of the Antioquia brown-banded antpitta was collected in 1878 by Thomas Knight Salmon, a British ornithologist, shortly before his death. It was taken from Santa Elena, just outside Medellín, on the route now between the city and its airport. Extensive habitat loss is thought to be the main factor behind its likely extinction. There was thick forest cover when the bird was found, but by the early 20th century the area had been subjected to widespread deforestation. Small patches of forest that do survive today are riddled with non-native species of pine and eucalyptus, which have changed the ecological balance since the antpitta was collected more than 120 years ago.

The bird is thought to be one of many types in the Central Andes where a species or sub-species occupies a specialist niche in a geographically small area. It lived in an area about 90 miles from the brown-banded antpitta's territory, and just about all that is known of its lifestyle is that it ate insects. Research into the bird's identity and its likely demise was conducted as part of the Project Biomap initiative to collate details on every specimen of bird from Colombia held in museums.

> The museum realised that they had a new type of antpitta on their hands, a subspecies of the brown-banded variety

Rediscovered Deer

A deer caught in a poacher's snare provided the first sighting of a species that had not been seen for almost eighty years. Members of an anti-poaching patrol came across the Sumatran muntjac, which was still alive, and were able to release it. The last known sighting of a Sumatran muntjac was in 1930, but photographs taken by the patrol prove it still exists. Shortly after the snared animal was freed, two others were pictured by infra-red camera traps that had been set up in another part of the Kerinci-Seblat National Park in western Sumatra.

Debbie Martyr of Fauna & Flora International took the photographs of the snared deer, *Muntiacus montanus*, while on a patrol in 2008 with the Kerinci-Seblat National Park Tiger Protection team. Close inspection of the pictures by Professor Colin Groves of the Australian National University later confirmed that the animal was the Sumatran muntjac. Taxonomists have now decided to classify the deer as a full species rather than a sub-species of the closely-related red muntjac.

The animal, which lives deep in the remote rainforests of Sumatra, was not discovered until 1914, and researchers know little about it. The original specimen of the deer was placed in the Raffles Museum in Singapore but was lost during the 1942 evacuation prior to the Japanese invasion.

Kerinci-Seblat National Park covers 5,400 sq.miles (14,000 sq.km) and is regarded as one of the world's biodiversity hotspots. Known inhabitants include 86 mammal species, 375 bird species and more than 4,000 types of plant. Scientists are convinced that much more remains to be discovered.

The Sumatran muntjac caught in a poacher's snare. The image was captured by a member of the anti-poaching patrol and provides proof that the deer still exists

The animal, which lives deep in the remote rainforests of Sumatra, was not discovered until 1914, and researchers knew little about it

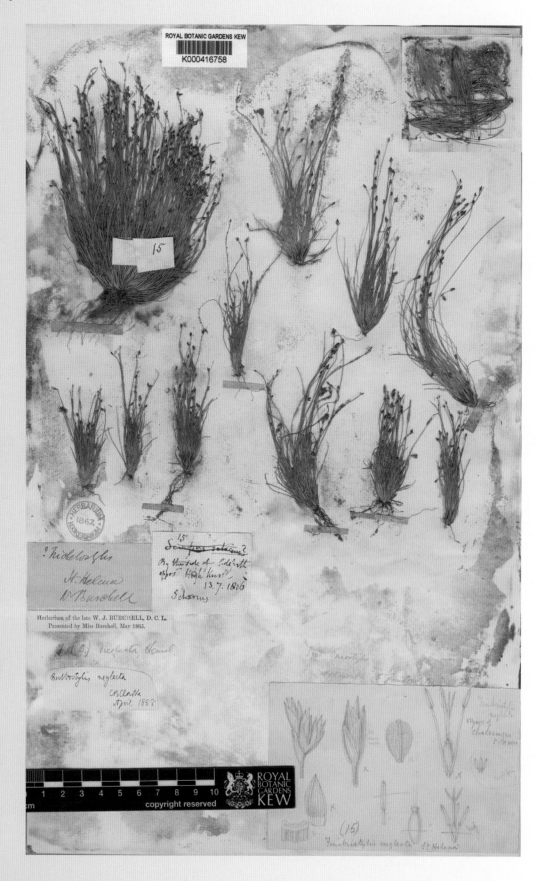

Clinging to Life

A tiny sedge thought to have been lost two centuries ago reappeared during work to save island plants from being overrun by invasive species. The neglected tuft sedge, *Bulbostylis neglecta* – so called because no one bothered to give it a name until it was rediscovered – grows on St Helena. It was recorded in 1806, nine years before Napoleon was exiled to the island after losing the Battle of Waterloo, but no one reported seeing it again until 200 years later when it was found clinging on to life at High Hill on the island.

Dr Phil Lambdon of the UK's Royal Botanic Gardens, Kew, came across the sedge by chance. He described it as "a dream discovery". Dr Lambdon recognised the plant because before setting out for the island he had looked through Kew's historic specimens which had been collected in the early nineteenth century by William Burchell, an explorer and naturalist. Burchell sailed to St Helena in 1805,

> **The species is so small there are still only enough to fill a sports bag**

remaining there until 1810, and the sedge was one of the plants he collected from the island in a spot overlooked by High Knoll Fort.

It was rediscovered during a survey of the island's vegetation by the South Atlantic Invasive Species Project as part of the research to establish ways to protect native species from being driven out by introduced plants and animals. With the survival of the sedge established, members of the South Atlantic Invasive Species Project conducted a more detailed search to find out how many there were. About 4,000 plants are now estimated to exist, but as the species is so small there are still only enough – should anyone try to pull them all out of the ground – to fill a sports bag.

St Helena itself was only discovered in 1502 but since then has suffered the extinction of seven species of bird and six plants found nowhere else in the world. A seventh plant, the St Helena Olive, *Nesiota elliptica*, has not been seen since 2004. Invasive plants and animals are a major cause of the extinctions, and the neglected tuft sedge is under threat of being overrun by an introduced African grass. Unless the spread of the grass can be halted the sedge will be gone in a decade. Claire Miller, of the Royal Society for the Protection of Birds, which manages the South Atlantic Invasive Species Project, said that though the sedge remains under threat of extinction, its rediscovery raises hopes that other species thought to have dis-appeared may yet still be found alive on the island "lurking in isolated spots".

opposite: **Sedge herbarium example from the 1800s before it was thought to be extinct**
left: **The rediscovered *Bulbostylis neglecta***

Behaviour
Alternative Lifestyles

Animal behaviour has been observed and studied by mankind for tens of thousands of years but many mysteries and surprises still remain. Instead of hunters trying to feed their families or augurs reading animal movements as messages from the gods, these days it is primarily scientists who are attempting to fathom the natural world. But whether the motivation for understanding wildlife is the pursuit of dinner or the pursuit of knowledge, the level of understanding can be so limited that researchers are still able to overturn popular assumptions about what animals do and why they do it. Even much-loved creatures that have been studied in detail over extended periods, such as cheetahs, can yield unexpected discoveries.

Cheating Cheetahs

Female cheetahs are the most unfaithful of the big cats to the point that they will risk their lives for an opportunity to cheat on their partners. They will risk deadly confrontations with lions and hyenas in their search for a second, third, fourth or even fifth male to sire cubs. Even if they escape attacks from rival predators, females determined to play the field dramatically increase their risk of getting parasites and diseases, especially sexually-transmitted diseases. Nevertheless, infidelity reaps huge benefits for female cheetahs, as it ensures that their cubs have a much wider genetic inheritance. Such promiscuous behaviour has the added bonus that the cubs are less likely to be attacked and killed by roving males. Because the female cheetah has travelled widely to offer her charms to several different mates, all of the males have a chance of being the father of the litter and have no desire to kill their own offspring.

Female cheetahs will risk their lives for an opportunity to cheat on their partners

Cheating cheetahs were identified among the cats living in a region of the Serengeti National Park in Tanzania. Droppings were collected by researchers and genetic material recovered from the faeces was used to determine the parenthood of each of the cubs. Analysis showed that 43 per cent of the forty-seven litters tested by the researchers contained cubs sired by at least two different fathers, and one litter of five cubs probably each had a different father. Cheetah cubs from the same litter can have different fathers because the mother ovulates each time she mates.

About a hundred cheetahs lived in the area where the study was carried out, though the females had access to males further afield because they were willing to travel so far. Cheetahs, *Acinonyx jubatus*, are unusual for a carnivore species in that the males have a fraction of the territory walked by the females. Males generally confine themselves to a territory of about 14 sq.miles (36 sq.km) whereas the females can have a home range of more than 300 sq.miles (777 sq.km).

Researchers involved in the study had suspected the females of infidelity but were astonished at the extent of it. It had always been assumed, as with many other species, that the males mated whenever they had the opportunity but the promiscuity among female cheetahs suggests that they are overcoming male attempts to monopolise those who are more sexually receptive. They are probably aided in this by the fact that they have much bigger territories to patrol. With fewer than 10,000 breeding cheetahs left in the wild, infidelity is thought to benefit the species as a whole because a higher number of males contribute to the gene pool.

The nine-year study was carried out by scientists from the Zoological Society of London (ZSL), the Wildlife Conservation Society in the US, and the Tanzania Wildlife Research Institute. Dada Gottelli, of ZSL, described the cheetahs as "the most unfaithful big cats" and said that the findings contradicted suggestions that the females were coy. She said the risks run by the females were, however, considerable. Their philandering increased the chances of meeting lions and hyenas, which would kill them if they had the opportunity, and it exposed them to a wider range of disease and parasites.

Sex War Arms Race

When a female diving beetle says no, she means never – to the point that she tries to evolve ever more effective defences against having to have sex. Acilius diving beetles are engaged in a sexual arms race that is driven by the unwillingness of the female to gratify the male's desire. So strong is the female's wish to be left alone that over time her body has adopted features that are designed specifically to shake off the male's attentions. This lack of co-operation means that the only way the diving beetle can succeed in procreating is through rape, and the males have been driven to evolve counter-measures to ensure they have a chance of holding on long enough to impregnate the female.

Neither courtship nor foreplay is in the male's repertoire as his sexual technique simply involves jumping onto a passing female and hanging on until she is too exhausted to resist. The female response when grabbed is to swim fast and erratically in an attempt to dislodge the unwanted suitor. Adaptations developed by the female to help her loosen the male's grip include ridges, hairs, furrows and depressions. In contrast, the males have evolved suction cups

Female *Acilius sinensiscalls*, displaying ridges which loosen the male's grip
opposite: **Male *Acilius sinensiscalls***

of different shapes and sizes to help them hold on to their reluctant partners.

Contrary to Charles Darwin's belief that the features on the female's back are designed to help the male grip, the furrows and other developments are in fact intended to help her escape. The constant demand for new means of defeating the opposite sex is believed to be the driving force in the evolution of new species of diving beetles. The Acilius genus, which is found across the northern hemisphere, has thirteen different species and researchers have charted the development of the sexual arms war by observing the arrangement of defences and countermeasures on them. It was demonstrated that the changes in the sucker cups are a response to the changes in the surface of the females' backs.

The separation of an Acilius beetle in Japan into two distinct species, *A. japonicus* and *A.*

Kishii, is thought to represent the most recent occasion when the changes became so extreme that a new beetle was created. It is calculated that it took place within the last few thousand generations. Dr Johannes Bergsten of the Natural History Museum and Imperial College both in London in the UK, traced the development of the arms race with Dr Kelly Miller of the University of New Mexico in the US. It was the first time the evolutionary battle of the sexes had been demonstrated across an entire genus. The researchers suggested that the more common means of sexual selection, in which males try to outdo one another and females choose the most successful males as mates, may be less of a gold standard set by nature than a technique that has emerged as an alternative to sexual conflict.

Tail-walking Dolphins

Wild dolphins have learned to tail-walk after one of their number witnessed captive animals performing the trick. At least three wild dolphins have learned how to perform the stunt in the water off Adelaide in Australia, and one of them likes to do it on the bow wave of large ships.

Tail-walking, while commonly taught to captive dolphins, is extremely rare in the wild except among the group off the coast of Adelaide. Scientists believe that a female bottlenose dolphin called Billie learned the trick in the 1980s when she spent three weeks in captivity.

Billie became trapped behind a marina lock and was captured for a dolphinarium where she lived before being released back into the wild. She was released before anyone could teach her tricks to entertain visitors but she has been seen tail-walking. Scientists think that she must have seen other dolphins carrying out the stunt, remembered what she had seen and worked out for herself how to do it once she was set free.

A second dolphin, Wave, has been observed tail-walking much more often than Billie. A third dolphin has also succeeded in performing the stunt. Scientists from the Whale and Dolphin Conservation Society were astonished at the tail-walking performances and are waiting to see if it is adopted by any more of the group. They have been unable to pinpoint why the dolphins should want to do it but suggest that it could be either a form of communication or a type of play.

Baby Talk

New research has shown that baby crocodiles are able to talk to their mothers before they have emerged from their eggs. The emit "Umph! umph! umph!" noises that roughly translate as "I'm ready to hatch, let's get out of here." By chattering shortly before they are due to make an appearance, they are telling their mothers that it is time to dig them out of the sand where the eggs were laid. Their siblings in other eggs in the nest probably also understand the calls, enabling the reptiles to co-ordinate their hatching. Researchers believe that such noises provide a living link with archosaurs, an ancient lineage of reptiles that gave rise to dinosaurs dating back 250 million years. .

Crocodiles and birds are both descended from the archosaurs – the birds through the dinosaurs – and have both inherited the ability to communicate from inside the egg. By communicating with their mothers and among themselves the infant reptiles maximise their chances of surviving the precarious first hours outside the egg. Even crocodiles are vulnerable when newly hatched but having a huge, fearsome mother on hand to

opposite: **Female Nile crocodile, *Crocodylus niloticus*, digging the sand in response to the playback of the calls of her young**
above: **Hatching crocodile babies**

act as bodyguard gives them protection from would-be predators as they clamber out of the sandy nest. Equally, the simultaneous appearance of all the baby crocodiles from a nest increases the chances

The calls enable the reptiles to co-ordinate their hatching

of survival because, even in the absence of their mother, there is protection in numbers. While some may fall victim to predators, the chances are that most will have time to get to cover. If they hatched separately they could be picked off one by one.

To find out if the noises made by crocodiles shortly before they hatch had any meaning, a group of researchers from France carried out a series of tests. They divided up crocodile eggs that were close to their expected hatching date into three groups. The noises made by hatchling crocodiles just before emerging from the egg were broadcast to one of the groups of eggs through loudspeakers. Many of the young animals answered back and all the eggs hatched during the playback or within ten minutes after it stopped. By contrast, meaningless noise played to a second group of eggs evoked little reaction. One hatched within minutes of the playback but none of the others emerged for at least another five hours.

To test the response of mother crocodiles to the noises, the researchers, from the Université Jean Monnet in France placed a speaker in the ground close to ten nests from which they had removed the eggs a few days earlier. Recordings of both pre-hatching calls and meaningless noises were played to the mothers. The adults moved in reaction to the pre-hatching calls far more frequently than to the other sounds, and eight of them began digging.

A baby crocodile hatching after hearing calls played by the buried loudspeaker

Beacons for Bees

Iridescence in flowers is largely unappreciated by the human eye but it acts as a beacon to bumblebees. It tells the bees just where to go to stock up on nectar and pollen, and is now seen as a common signpost put up by flowers rather than as an incidental feature of garden blooms.

Researchers studying the hibiscus found that a series of waxy lines on the petals were responsible for the flower's iridescence. Once they had worked out the role of the waxy lines the scientists realised that they had seen similar features on other flowers. Further investigation quickly determined that several other plants had similar lines – including buttercups, legumes, evening primroses and asters – and whilst the iridescence is invisible to humans, it is easily seen by bumblebees.

Scientists from the University of Cambridge and Queen Mary University of London in the UK performed a series of tests which showed that

Iridescence is invisible to humans but easily seen by bees

bees can learn to tell which hues lead to nectar and pollen and which should be ignored. Iridescent discs were topped with a container filled with sweet-tasting sucrose for the tests, while non-iridescent discs were covered with containers filled with quinine, which tastes very bitter to bees. Most bumblebees learnt quickly that they would be much better rewarded if they flew to the iridescent discs.

The precisely arranged lines of a waxy secretion on the petals cause certain wavelengths of light to rebound. The colour rebounding can vary depending on the angle of approach so that the shading changes as the bees move about. According to Dr Beverley Glover of the University of Cambridge, initial findings suggest that iridescence is widespread in flowers and insects like the bumblebee are much better equipped to see it than humans.

opposite: **Bumblebee landing on a flower** above: **Bees learning to associate the iridescence of epoxy replica flowers with a reward**

Gone Fishing

Wolves may be fearsome hunters, but given the choice they would often rather go fishing. Deep in the Canadian forests of British Columbia wolves have learnt to take advantage of the annual salmon run. They will stand in the river with their heads hung low and when a wolf spies a suitable fish it will dash forward and plunge its head into the water to grab a meal in its jaws. For most of the year deer make up 90 to 95 per cent of the wolves' diet but for several weeks in the early autumn this falls substantially as they turn to fish.

During the salmon season at least 40 per cent of the wolves' diet comprises fish, and in some packs it makes up almost 70 per cent. Dr Chris Darimont of the University of Victoria in Canada said the change from the usual diet made great sense for the wolves, *Canis lupus*. Bite for bite, the salmon offer slightly more protein, much more fat and provide the wolves with four times more calories than deer. Equally, the fish are an easy meal in comparison with deer which range over wide areas and can be hard to locate, even before they can be chased and brought down.

It was calculated that the wolves need an average of 6lbs (2.7kg) of deer meat each day to survive, but the nutritional value of the pink salmon is so high that the predators need only eat 1.4lbs (0.62kg) of fish a day. Salmon have the added advantage of being a much less dangerous prey than deer, which will kick out when attacked and frequently leave wolves with serious or fatal injuries from smashed ribs or cracked skulls. To the surprise of researchers, once the fish were caught the wolves only ate the heads, which meant they needed to catch 4.6 fish each day to meet their nutritional requirements. It was speculated that wolves had learnt to avoid the rest of the body because of the risk of picking up parasites.

Wolves had been known previously to take the occasional fish but the study, which included researchers from the Raincoast Conservation Foundation and the University of Calgary, both in Canada, revealed that wolves seek out salmon in preference to other prey, rather than eating it simply because deer are absent. The wolves that

have shown a preference for fish over deer live in a remote coastal area of forest in western British Columbia that, with little logging and few roads, is rarely reached by people.

Brown and black bears were seen to fish the same estuary system as the wolves, and the animals occasionally came into conflict, but on many other occasions the carnivores seemed to tolerate one another from a distance. Wolves, however, steered clear of fishing in the Neekas River which has the highest intensity of salmon. Researchers suggested that so many bears fished this waterway that wolves would have come into conflict with them if they tried to compete for the salmon there. Bears display a more effective fishing technique as they are able to hook salmon out of the water with their claws instead of having to plunge their heads under the surface.

When a wolf spies a suitable fish it plunges its head into the water to grab a meal in its jaws

Researchers were able to establish the importance of fish in the diet of the wolves in a 1,351 sq. mile (3,500 sq.km) area around Bella Bella in British Columbia by analysing the content of their faeces. Analysis of the isotopic content of clumps of fur shed by the animals provided further indications of what the wolves had eaten over the previous six months. Eight groups of wolves were studied for the four-year project, and one of the highlights for researchers was being able to watch cubs learn to fish. The cubs would frequently slip on algae-covered rocks and repeatedly miss the salmon. Once they got the knack of seizing a fish from the river the cubs would proudly show off their catches to the parents and siblings.

A wolf fishing in Brooks River Falls, Katmai National Park & Preserve, Alaska

Bugs in Bed

Bedbug sex is so violent and dangerous that the females have developed a unique organ to improve their chances of surviving the ordeal. The immune organ gives the females a concentrated form of immunity against infections introduced during mating. Extra protection against infections is necessary for bedbugs because the male's sexual technique is as unhygienic as it is unattractive.

Rather than making use of the female genitalia, the male bedbug wields its penis like a dagger and simply stabs its unwilling partner in the abdomen. Bedbugs inhabit many dirty and unsanitary places so infections are regularly introduced by the penis into the wound. This unconventional sexual technique is thought to explain why female bedbugs suffer a 25 per cent higher mortality rate than the males. This rate would be even even higher if the immune organ hadn't evolved. It provides a reservoir of white blood cells which act as the first line of defence against infection caused when the penis pierces the abdomen and introduces bacteria and fungi.

The immune organ was originally observed by naturalists 200 years ago but scientists were mystified as to what it was until Professor Mike Siva-Jothy of the University of Sheffield in the UK recognised it as an organ and realised it was a concentrated immunity system. He announced the discovery of the identity and function of the organ to the Royal Entomological Society in the UK and described the sexual practices of bedbugs as so extreme that the system is likely to have evolved just the once.

Their unsavoury habits, however, may eventually result in scientific advances as the organ offers researchers a fresh opportunity to investigate insect immunity. Until now, insect immune systems have proved a challenging subject to study because the immunity is spread through the body, but in the female bedbug it can now be studied in a concentrated form. By learning how immunity works in an insect it could be possible to devise methods to prevent mosquitoes and other insects passing diseases such as malaria to people.

Despite the brutality of bedbug courtship and mating, the male's semen succeeds in migrating through the body to reach and fertilise the eggs. The females are seemingly reluctant participants in the reproductive process – they only mate after a meal when they swell up by 30 per cent and are so engorged that they cannot escape the attentions of the male.

> Female bedbugs have developed a unique organ to improve their chances of surviving sex

As busy as a...Sloth

Sloths may live life in the slow lane but when it comes to laziness they have been condemned unfairly. The animals are known for their slow movement and their seemingly inexhaustible desire to sleep, but data provided by electronic tags has overturned the notion that sloths laze away the greater part of the day. Instead of spending almost sixteen hours of every day fast asleep, as studies of captive animals had shown, when they are in the wild they sleep for just 9.6 hours in every twenty-four. For the rest of the day, far from being slothful, they are active as they clamber around the rainforest, mostly in the canopies where they are safest, searching for food and trying to keep out of the way of predators.

Researchers measured activity levels by attaching miniaturised electroencephalogram tags to brown-throated three-toed sloths, *Bradypus variegatus*. The tags recorded the activity levels in the brains of three female sloths and indicated whether the animals were asleep or awake. Analysis of the data recorded by the tags, which were removed after after three days on one of the animals and after five days on two of them, showed that the sloths stayed awake for 15.85 hours each day. Sleep could take place at any time of the day or night, but it was observed that the sloths were usually asleep during the last part of the night, having spent the first two-thirds foraging.

Dr Niels Rattenborg of the Max Planck Institute for Ornithology in Germany led the study and was confident that the six-hour difference between sleeping patterns in captive and wild sloths has implications for the importance and function of sleep. The study suggested that in the wild the animals slept for as little as they could without damaging their efficiency when awake. It also suggested that the research based on sleep in captive animals needed to be reassessed.

Tags were attached to sloths living on the Smithsonian Tropical Research Institute's Barro Colorado Island in Panama where they lived mainly on a diet of leaves from 28 species of tree and three species of lianas. The sloths had to remain vigilant to avoid being eaten by either ocelots, *Leopardus pardalis*, or pumas, *Puma concolor*, the main predators on the island. Locator tags were attached to the sloths so that the animals could be found again and the electronic devices removed. After three months the sloths were tracked down to make sure that they remained in good health and were not affected by the study. Researchers taking part included scientists from the University of Ulm in Germany, the University of Zurich in Switzerland, and Princeton University in the US.

Observations of sloths in London Zoo supported the idea that boredom is one of the main reasons that captive sloths spend much longer dozing. Keepers had noticed that when sloths were introduced to a new, open-plan area designed to let animals roam in a rainforest-like habitat they became much more active than when confined to traditional enclosures. Tai Strike, a veterinary officer for the Zoological Society of London, said that the old idea that all sloths needed to keep them happy was a tree to hang from and a ready supply of food was a misconception.

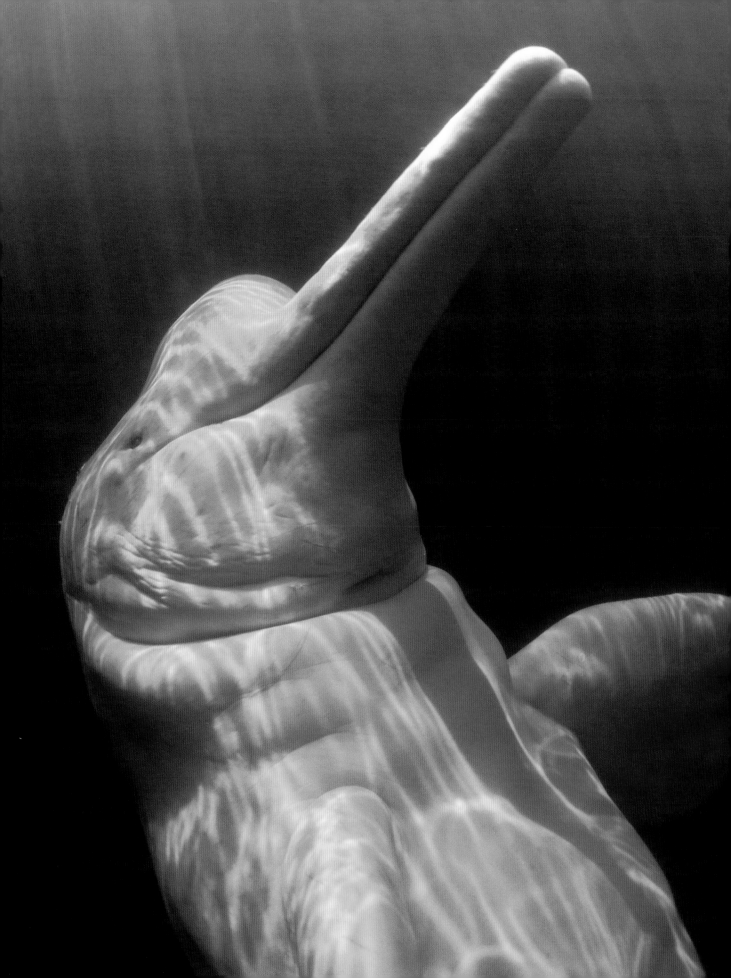

Say it with Weeds

Weeds, branches and lumps of clay have been found to be the romantic dolphin's equivalent of courting with chocolates and flowers. Male river dolphins, or botos, in the Amazon and Orinoco display the objects in their mouths and use them to thrash the water in what is thought to be an attempt to impress the females. The courtship displays can, however, stir up trouble among other male botos and can provoke aggressive attacks on the object carriers.

Object carrying was previously thought to be an example of the playfulness of dolphins but researchers have now found that it is far more likely to be linked to mating rituals. Scientists observed the use of objects in 221 out of 6,026 groups of botos known to inhabit the Amazon and Orinoco river systems in South America. The botos, *Inia geoffrensis*, were far more likely to grab hold of objects when females were about and the practice was almost exclusively conducted by adult males.

Clumps of grass floating on the surface of the river were usually selected to impress the females. They made up 40 per cent of the objects used in the displays, while branches or sticks made up 24 per cent. Lumps of clay from the river bed accounted for 36 per cent. The behaviour was identified by an Anglo-Brazilian team of scientists who spent three years studying it at the Mamirauá Reserve, a flooded rainforest in Brazil.

Professor Tony Martin of St Andrews University in the UK said the river dolphins would rise to the surface with weeds or other objects in the mouths, often while adopting a vertical position and rotating as they sank back into the water. They would often throw or slap the object against the surface of the river. Fights would break out among males close to the display and researchers established that when one of the botos was displaying weeds or another object, aggressive behaviour was forty times more likely than when none had a display object. The types of aggressive behaviour seen by the researchers included leaping onto another boto, biting, lunging and hitting another individual with the head or tail.

It was Professor Martin, along with Dr Vera da Silva of the National Institute for Amazonian Research in Brazil, who realised that the objects were carried as part of a courtship ritual rather than play. They have been studying the river dolphins since 1994 as part of Project Boto, a research initiative aimed at helping protect the animal. They were joined in the study of object carrying by Dr Peter Rothery of the Centre for Ecology and Hydrology in the UK.

There are thought to be tens of thousands of botos in South America but their numbers are falling fast and researchers are increasingly concerned about the dolphins' survival prospects. Pollution and fishing are the biggest threats, as the botos are used as bait for catching piracatinga, a type of fish.

> Male botos thrash weeds, branches and lumps of clay in the water to impress females

Chattering Ants and the Cuckoo Caterpillar

A caterpillar has learnt to talk like a queen in its quest for an easy life in the heart of an ant colony. Caterpillars from Rebel's large blue butterfly, *Maculinea rebeli*, imitate queen ants to ensure they are treated like royalty. Their ability to copy the noises made by queens was uncovered as researchers discovered that ants routinely talk to each other inside the nest. The finding explained why it is that ants of the species *Myrmica schencki* give the caterpillars priority treatment even over the safety of their own larvae.

To get into the colony and win protection the caterpillars secrete a chemical cocktail and engage in begging behaviour to convince the ants to look after them. But it remained a mystery as to why they should get preferential treatment until it was realised they mimic the noises made

by the queen ants. Mimicry allows the butterflies' developing young to conceal the fact that they are interlopers from their hosts, and also ensures that they are treated like royalty. The noises are convincing enough to persuade the worker ants to give them the best treatment, which can even include killing and feeding them the ants' own larvae when food is scarce, said Dr Karsten Schönrogge of the Centre for Ecology & Hydrology in the UK. They are originally carried into the nests by the ants after eating the flowers of gentian plants, and they are so successful as mimics that when the colony is in danger, the worker ants will rescue the caterpillars first.

During their time in the nests the caterpillars gain 98 per cent of their final weight before turning into pupae and then butterflies. Rebel's large blue butterfly is an endangered species, living only in a handful of meadows in mountain regions of Europe, but is one of an estimated 10,000 invertebrate species which are ant parasites.

The discovery that sound plays a role within the nests may help explain how many of the parasitical species take advantage of their hosts. It was made possible by miniaturisation and advances in audio technology which enabled scientists to make the first recordings of ants talking to each other. The recordings suggest that sound plays a much more important role in ant communication than previously suspected. It was

realised more than 40 years ago that ants had a natural built-in plectrum and washboard in their abdomens which they rubbed together to make an alarm call, but only with the application of recent developments in audio technology has it become possible to record the sounds within nests and to realise that the noises are more than just simple alarm calls.

One of the first ant sounds to be interpreted was a noise made by the queen which prompted all her nearby subjects to stand to attention. When they heard the queen the other ants would stand motionless, often for hours, with their jaws open and antennae pushed outwards. Any creature that got too close while they were in the 'en garde' position would be attacked.

Miniature loud speakers were placed inside nests and were used to play recordings of queens, enabling researchers to talk back to the insects. It was observed that one of the responses generated by the playbacks was for ants to press their antennae against the speakers just as they would to greet each other. It was the first time that researchers were able to demonstrate that different sounds within the ant nest would provoke different responses. Dr Francesca Barbero of the University of Turin in Italy said it showed that the use of sound to exchange information between ants had been greatly underestimated. The sounds were made by the ants scraping the natural plectrum across the file, the pars stridens – a natural 'washboard'. On the queen ants the pars stridens was 44 per cent longer and with gaps between ridges 33 per cent wider than on the workers. Professor Jeremy Thomas, of the University of Oxford in the UK, said further research should establish how wide a vocabulary ants have and to what extent they rely on sound to communicate.

opposite: **worker attends to Maculinea larvae**
above: **ants around Maculinea pupa**

Red Rag to an Elephant

Centuries of having sharp spears hurled at them by Maasai warriors have taught elephants to beware of red clothing. The animals are colour-blind and see red as a drab hue yet still seem to be able to distinguish it from other colours, living up to their reputation of never forgetting.

When they come across old red clothing that has been worn by a member of the Maasai people in Kenya they display signs of fear and nervousness, and run away. An article of white clothing worn by the Kamba tribe, a crop-growing people, provokes a much less fearful response. The African elephants ran further and faster from a Maasai's clothing than from a Kamba's and would take much longer to calm down afterwards.

The discovery indicated that over the years the elephants had learnt to associate red clothing with Maasai warriors, who traditionally wear red, and for whom a long-standing test of manhood is to spear an elephant. Researchers investigating the ability of elephants to distinguish between different groups of people found that the animals used both sight and their sense of smell. By sniffing the garments they were able to tell whether the clothing had been discarded by a member of the Maasai or the Kamba peoples.

Tests showed that their sense of smell is so acute that they could tell which tribe the clothes belonged to from a distance of 330ft (100m) or more. When presented with clean clothing that had never been worn, however, the elephants still reacted when the fabrics were red. Clean, unused white garments prompted only mild curiosity whereas clean, unused red clothing provoked an aggressive reaction including stamping their feet, raising their trunks and lowering their heads. Their sense of smell told them there were no Maasai in the vicinity, which explained why they did not flee.

According to the researchers, Dr Lucy Bates and Professor Richard Byrne of St Andrews University, the study demonstrated that elephants were clearly able to distinguish between the two peoples and the threat posed by each of them.

above left: **Elephants fleeing the scent of Maasai people on an experimental track**
above right: **A Maasai in traditional dress**

A Wolf in Dog's Clothing

Wolves with black coats have been found to owe their colour to domestic dogs in an intriguing example of genetic role reversal. Dogs have long been known to have descended from wolves, but it has now been found that they returned the compliment with a genetic inheritance that is helping wolves to survive in modern times.

Despite their colour the black wolves prowling the Canadian forests are the same species as the grey predators, *Canis lupus*. Their fur, however, is much darker, and since more than half of the wolves in the forests are now black, the colour is proving to be a successful survival trait. The colour derives from a mutated gene which first appeared among domestic dogs that are thought to have reached North America with their human masters about 14,000 years ago. As people walked into the continent over the Bering Strait they brought their dogs with them, and one or more of those with the black fur gene interbred with grey wolves.

Over the millennia the black fur is assumed to have conferred a slight advantage, and today more than half of the wolves in the boreal forests of Canada are black. The dogs that passed on the gene, however, are thought to have died out. Domestic dogs in North America today derive from other stocks. Professor Marco Musiani, of the University of Calgary in Canada, said the black fur was the first example of genetic engineering in wolves that has been caused by human actions.

Wolves are thought to have inherited black coats from domestic dogs

Researchers have yet to explain fully why the colour aids wolf survival in the forests, but as 62 per cent of the wolves are black it is regarded as too much of a coincidence for it not to be an advantage.

One possible factor is that the coat colour gene, beta-defensin, is from a family of genes that have been linked to the ability to fight off infections. Scientists believe the black colouration may help wolves adapt to changes in the environment brought about by human activity. In particular, they think that as climate change causes the Arctic tundra habitat to retreat, the black-coated wolves will be better adapted to the new conditions.

below: **62 per cent of wolves in the boreal forests of Canada now have black coats, as opposed to the ancestral grey**

From Dung Collector to Hunter Killer

A dung beetle has been found which has turned exclusively to predation rather than munching on its traditional fare. It has ditched its peaceful lifestyle to hunt and butcher millipedes laced with toxins. It is the only one of an estimated 5,000 scarab beetles in the world that has evolved to track and kill other animals. The switch from being one of nature's refuse collectors to becoming a specialist killer has been described by scientists as "a remarkable transition".

The species, *Deltochilum valgum*, inhabits forest undergrowth in Peru and probably developed a taste for flesh because of the huge competition among invertebrates for dung. Other dung beetles around the world are known to scavenge decaying flesh but the Peruvian species has gone one step further by actively seeking out and killing other animals. It is thought to prey exclusively on toxic millipedes and shows a strong preference for live but injured prey, possibly because the chemicals released by open wounds makes them easier to sniff out.

Tiny changes in the beetle's anatomy have turned it into a dangerous foe for millipedes, which can be as much as ten times bigger than

> **The beetle has ditched dung to hunt and butcher toxic millipedes**

their killers. Captured millipedes refuse to give in without a fight and can be seen writhing madly in an attempt to drag themselves free when caught by the beetle. Once the beetle has managed to grab a millipede it hangs on grimly until its prey is too exhausted to resist any longer, and then moves in for the coup de grâce. Once the prey has been subdued, the beetle moves towards the front and inserts its mouth parts into a gap in the millipede's exoskeleton to lever off its head. The mouth parts are specially adapted to despatching and devouring prey as they are narrower than those of the dung-eating species, and are better suited to finding their way into tiny gaps in the exoskeleton. Once the millipede is dead the killer beetle drags it away – with the help of an elongated hind leg – to a suitable spot where it cuts it up and eats the soft inner flesh, picking the hard outer shell clean and scattering the dismembered pieces under dead leaves.

The beetle's predatory habits were documented by a team of Canadian and US researchers, led by Dr Trond Larsen of Princeton University, who had previously observed it

carrying dead millipedes. The transition from dung collector to killer is regarded by researchers as a prime example of how animals evolve to occupy new niches under the pressure of intense competition. It remains easily identifiable as a species of dung beetle but the small differences in its anatomy are perfect for its new lifestyle.

Scientists involved in the study identified the creature's behaviour after using pitfall traps to collect 102,639 dung beetles from 102 species. In a series of tests, dead millipedes were found to attract 35 species of dung beetle, whereas live millipedes attracted only five species. Four of these were also attracted to dung, carrion and other types of bait but *D. valgum* approached only millipedes. Two other species of dung beetles have previously been observed preying on queen leaf-cutter ants but they also fed on dung and carrion. It is thought that the predatory dung beetle is able to eat the millipedes because the toxins have little or no effect on it. The millipedes developed the poison glands as a means of discouraging larger predators, such as mammals and birds, on which they would be effective.

Life in the Fast Lane

A chameleon which dies of old age at just five months has been identified as the shortest-lived vertebrate on land. Labord's chameleon has such an extreme life cycle that it spends more time in the egg than out of it. Many plants and insects are annuals but the chameleon, *Furcifer labordi*, is the first tetrapod – four-limbed vertebrates that include mammals, birds and reptiles – found to complete its entire life cycle within a year. Other short-lived tetrapods include nine marsupials and eleven reptiles, but though most individuals in each species die within the year, some members manage to last a little longer.

Each generation of Labord's chameleons starts emerging in November. In less than five months even those that have survived disease and predators die of old age. Death for the chameleons, found in the arid south-west region of Madagascar, is a synchronised event as all die within a few days of each other. Once the frenzied mating season is over, the lizards start losing weight, becoming slower and weaker. Some of them decline so rapidly that they fall out of trees like autumn leaves.

During their short lives the chameleons have to eat voraciously to enable them to grow rapidly to full, adult size in the space of two months. The breakneck pace of life is maintained into the breeding season, when the animals are so aggressive in their desire to mate that fights between rivals can end in death. Egg-laying mostly takes place in February and the embryos develop over the next eight to nine months. Once hatched, they live for four to five months. Hatchlings are never alive at the same time as adults.

The researchers who identified the annual life cycle observed that the chameleon's life history is more akin to that of insects and aquatic vertebrates than its own close relatives. Quite why the animal has such a truncated life cycle is not known, but the harsh environment may be a significant factor.

The species suffers high losses from predators, and if it did live all year round it would face severe difficulties in coping with the desert scrubland in the driest region of Madagascar. The animal's small size, short life and early sexual maturity provide it with effective counter measures for the species to survive. Brevity of life in the natural habitat could, the researchers have suggested, offer a possible explanation for the notorious difficulty in keeping some species of chameleon alive in captivity. Rather than suffering from inexplicably inappropriate conditions the captive animals could simply be biologically programmed to die young.

The research was carried out by Dr Kristopher Karsten, of Oklahoma State University and scientists from the American Museum of Natural History both in the US, and the University of Antananarivo in Madagascar. Chameleons were captured at night while sleeping and then released within twenty-four hours of being measured and observed. Seven of the animals were fitted with a radio transmitter to allow the researchers to find and measure them every day. Dr Karsten said that the "remarkable" life of Labord's chameleon and its longer-lived relatives could in the future provide insights into the genes and hormones that determine longevity in humans.

Multilingual Bees

Honeybees have developed a talent for languages that allows them to interpret what other species are saying. This ability was discovered when scientists realised that different dialects have been established among the nine species of honeybee. Dancing enables honeybees to tell each other where to go to find food, water or new nesting sites, and recent studies have uncovered differences between the dance movements of each of the species. The duration and orientation of waggles made by the bees in their dances indicate the distance and direction of food. Researchers from Australia, China and Germany have found that the duration of the waggles, and thus their meaning, varies among the different species.

Experiments conducted in China have revealed that European and Asian honeybees, *Apis mellifera lingustica* and *Apis cerana cerana*, can understand what the other is saying well enough to communicate and cooperate. To conduct the tests honeybees from one species were introduced into the hives of other species, a task that proved something of a challenge as the usual response of a bee to finding a "foreigner" in the hive is to attack and kill it.

Asian and European bees, the most distant of the nine species geographically, proved to be the most compatible, and after several abortive and murderous episodes, they were finally induced to live in harmony for more than fifty days. According to Dr Shaowu Zhang of the Australian National University, such mixed species colonies allowed the team to observe the bees closely and to establish that, despite honeybee language being among the most studied forms of animal communication, surprises are still possible.

Poison Dragon

Venom powerful enough to kill or incapacitate large prey has been found to be part of the Komodo dragon's lethal armoury. The discovery overturns a popular belief that one of the ways the Komodo dragon, *Varanus komodoensis*, killed its prey was to infect it with bacteria from its mouth. This finding has helped an international team of researchers to conclude that the giant ripper lizard, a close but extinct relative of the Komodo dragon, was probably the largest venomous lizard ever to have lived. Researchers from institutions in Australia, the US, the UK, Chile, China, Singapore, Switzerland, Belgium, Israel and the Netherlands took part in the study to assess the Komodo dragon's armoury.

Researchers discovered that the Komodo dragons, the heaviest lizards alive today, are venomous when they subjected the skull of one of the animals to close analysis. A CT scan revealed the existence of glands and ducts in the animal's lower jaw, and samples taken from a captive dragon revealed that these are loaded with toxins. Scientists concluded that the venom is one of the animal's most important means of bringing down prey. Analysis confirmed that the Komodo dragon has a much weaker bite than a crocodile, and that the design of the skull meant a more muscular bite would result in stress damage.

The bite of the saltwater crocodile, *Crocodylus porosus*, was measured and compared to that of the Komodo dragon and was found to be over six times more powerful. A comparatively weak bite, especially when prey is twisting and turning, limits the dragon's ability to overwhelm

animals by tearing off chunks of flesh, but its jaws are ideal for pulling. By pulling prey, or by holding its ground while prey tries to escape by pulling away, the Komodo dragon inflicts deep lacerations in the animal it has seized – scientists have dubbed this the "grip and rip" technique. Wounds caused by the predatory lizards, which live in Indonesia, can be so severe that the victim bleeds to death, but the venom gives the dragons an even greater chance of making a successful kill.

Scientists investigating the venom found that, like the poisons used by snakes, it contains a complex variety of proteins. Many of the toxins are associated with effects such as preventing blood from clotting, muscle paralysis, and inducing shock and low blood pressure. The likely effects suggested by the chemical composition of the venom matched observations in the wild, as the prey appeared unusually quiet after being bitten and rapidly went into shock. Similarly, they were consistent with anecdotal reports, and the observations of Dr Bryan Fry of the University of Melbourne in Australia, who noticed the difficulty of stopping bleeding in humans who had been bitten by the dragon.

In addressing what they saw as the myth that prey can be killed by bacteria introduced by bites, the researchers concluded that such a method was unlikely, as other studies had failed to detect any especially deadly bacteria consistently present in the mouths of the dragons. It was previously widely believed that infected prey would be tracked by the dragons until, hours or perhaps days later, they died or were too weak to flee. One of the reasons the venomous qualities of the dragons were missed by researchers in the past was that the teeth lacked the grooves which in other poisonous animals are used to channel toxins into a wound.

Komodo dragons can weigh more than 200lbs (91kg) making them the heaviest lizards alive today. They are arguably the largest, although there is one species, the crocodile monitor, that grows longer – 15ft (4.5m) compared to the dragon's 10ft (3m).

The Komodo dragons are closely related to the much larger but extinct giant ripper lizard, *V. prisca*, which died out in Australia about 40,000 years ago. It was previously estimated to be more than 23ft (7m) long and almost 4,410lbs (2,000kg) in weight, but the team investigating the Komodo dragon gave a more conservative minimum estimate of 18ft (5.5m) long and 1,268lbs (575kg) in weight.

The giant ripper lizard was also concluded to be toxic because of its close relationship with the dragon and the fact snakes and venomous lizards have a common origin. Having poison as a weapon makes it much more likely to have been a predator than a scavenger.

> The extinct giant ripper lizard, a relative of the komodo, was probably the largest venomous lizard ever

above: **CT scans of a komodo skull revealed the existence of venom glands and ducts in the lower jaw**

Deep Sea Life

Some of the deepest living fish on the planet were filmed for the first time when a camera was sent almost 5 miles (8km) beneath the waves. Scientists monitoring the images were fascinated to see snailfish acting sociably on the sea floor as they fed at depths of 25,260ft (7,700m). It had been anticipated that at such depths food would be in such short supply that fish would be forced to live as slow-moving loners, but to the astonishment of researchers the footage recorded by cameras fixed to a deep sea submersible revealed that snailfish congregate to feed, possibly even in family groups. Moreover, instead of living life in slow motion to make the most of limited energy reserves, the fish demonstrated that they are active swimmers.

The film showed a 17-strong shoal of a deep-living species of snailfish, *Pseudoliparis amblystomopsis*, feeding on tiny shrimps that were scavenging on a corpse. At such depths the animals live in complete darkness, so instead of depending on sight the snailfish have vibration receptors in their snouts to detect food and to avoid collisions with any obstacles in their path. The species was familiar to scientists but previous observations had been of specimens in poor condition that had been brought to the surface.

At the depth at which the snailfish were observed on film the water pressure is huge – 5,000 tons per sq.in (7,900 tons per sq.m) – so they have special adaptations that enable them to live under such conditions. Unmanned submersibles are used to give researchers a glimpse of life in the depths of the sea. The snailfish, which were filmed in the Japan Trench in the North-West Pacific, were so deep down that it took the marine vehicles five hours to descend to the bottom. The machines, which used a sheet of sapphire in the windows in place of glass to cope with the pressure, remained in the depths for two days before being given the signal to surface.

The fish were discovered as part of the HADEEP project of the University of Aberdeen's Oceanlab in the UK and the University of Tokyo's Ocean Research Institute in Japan. The prime purpose of the project is to investigate what is in the seas below 20,000ft (6,000m), in the hadal zone, where it is perpetually dark. Hadal snailfish live in many of the trenches beneath the Pacific but different species are found in – and are confined to – each region. The deepest a fish is known to live is 27,467ft (8,372m), where a type of cusk eel called *Abyssobrotula galatheae* was found. It died when taken to the surface.

In another expedition, researchers from France managed to collect a zoarcid fish, *Pachycara saldanhai*, from 7,546ft (2,300m) deep on the Mid-Atlantic Ridge and kept it alive when they brought it to the surface. This was 3,117ft (950m) deeper than the level from which any fish had been brought up alive previously. It was able to survive the ascent because it was trapped in a prototype container designed to maintain specimens at the same pressure as when they were caught. Using the device in 2006 at two hydrothermal vent fields, the zoarcid fish and more than 150 shrimps were caught and brought alive to the surface. Two species of shrimp were caught at 5,577ft (1,700m), *Mirocaris fortunata* and *Chorocaris chacei*, and a third, *Rimicaris exoculata*, was retrieved from the same depth as the zoarcid fish.

Dr Bruce Shillito of the Université Pierre et Marie Curie said that it is hard to recover live fish from below 3,280ft (1,000m), but he hoped that the pressurised device would allow scientists to study deep sea species in laboratories and thus gain a better understanding of them.

Boozy Shrew

A tiny treeshrew with a taste for alcohol has been found to drink so much so often that it should spend most of its life in a haze. Pentailed treeshrews frequently sup from bertam palms, which produce a potent nectar as strong as beer. A human attempting, size for size, to keep up with this denizen of the Malaysian rainforest would quickly find himself with a life-threatening chronic alcohol problem. But for the nocturnal treeshrew the alcoholic nectar is its main source of nourishment, and researchers failed to find any sign of drunkenness or hangovers in the tiny primate. Scientists concluded that the pentailed treeshrew, *Ptilocercus lowii*, is equipped with special adaptations that allow it to drink without ill effect. What those mechanisms are, however, has yet to be identified.

> The alcoholics nectar is its main source of nourishment

Seven other mammals, such as the slow loris and the plantain squirrel, drink from the flowers of the bertam palm daily, but the pentailed treeshrews are by far the heaviest drinkers. They consume so much nectar that, were their reactions to alcohol similar to humans, they would be falling over drunk every three days – suicidal behaviour in the wild with so many predators about.

The treeshrew weighs just 47 g. By comparison an adult woman would have to drink nine glasses of wine in twelve hours to match its consumption. On average, the treeshrew drinks from the bertam palm for 138 minutes every night, while slow lorises manage 86 minutes. The alcoholic nectar attracts a variety of animals to the bertam palm, *Eugeissona tristis*, and in return for sustenance the drinkers unwittingly act as pollinators.

At its strongest the nectar had an alcoholic content of 3.8 per cent and, apart from the fruit pulp of one other wild plant, it is the strongest to occur naturally in a food. The alcoholic content of the nectar varies but is strongest immediately after being exuded by the plant's buds, which are miniature fermenting chambers. Once exuded, the alcoholic concentration begins to fall, in part due to evaporation. To get at the nectar the treeshrew scampers up and down the stemless palm licking the flower buds – each of the plants has on average more than a thousand flowers.

Pentailed treeshrews are thought to be the closest living animal to the primates that lived in the rainforests 55 million years ago. The international research team believes that the animal's relationship with alcohol could provide insights into drinking among humans. Treeshrews and people are thought to have a common ancestor from 55 million years ago and according to the researchers, led by Dr Frank Wiens of Bayreuth University in Germany, it is likely that primates had by then already been exposed to potentially harmful levels of alcohol. Dr Wiens hopes that by learning more about the treeshrew and other mammals that use the palm as a feeding station fresh insights can be gained into the importance of alcohol to humans, who only learnt the art of brewing about 9,000 years ago.

The Early Bird Catches the Mate

Miniaturised electronic trackers have revealed that songbirds on migration fly more than three times as fast as suspected. Small migratory songbirds were thought to have been limited to about 93 miles (150km) a day, but geolocators have shown they can manage more than 310 miles (500km).

One bird, a purple martin, astonished researchers by taking just 13 days to fly 4,660 miles (7,500km) from Brazil to its Cambridge Springs breeding grounds in Pennsylvania in the US. Data from the study showed that the birds show a much greater sense of urgency when heading towards their breeding grounds than when they are flying south for the winter. The spring migration was at least twice as fast, and up to six times quicker than the more relaxed southwards journey later in the year.

These findings are the result of a study led by Professor Bridget Stutchbury of York University in Canada in which miniature geolocators were fitted like backpacks to 34 songbirds to assess their flight performance. A variety of other techniques had been used in the past to establish the distance and routes flown by migratory birds, but the lightweight geolocators allowed researchers to accurately track songbirds for the first time. The light-sensitive geolocators, developed by the British Antarctic Survey, recorded the time of dawn and sunset each day. This allowed researchers to work out the position of the birds as it provided daily locations for each of those wearing the coin-sized backpack. The geolocators were fitted using teflon straps looped around the legs of 20 purple martins, *Progne subis*, and 14 wood thrushes, *Hylocichla mustelina*; both common birds in the US. The devices were placed at the base of the birds' backs and were carried like a backpack. The coin-sized tracker weighed just 0.035 of an ounce (half a gram) which meant the birds could carry them without their survival prospects being significantly impaired.

Birds were trapped and fitted with the devices in Pennsylvania in 2007 shortly before they flew south for the winter. Nine of the birds are known to have returned in the spring of 2008 and seven of the devices were recovered – five from wood thrushes and two from purple martins. Analysis of the readings recorded by the geolocators enabled the research team to work out the routes the birds had taken on their migrations, where they wintered, how frequent long stops were, and how quickly they were travelling.

Purple martins, which are active during the day and prefer grassland habitats, and wood thrushes, a night-flying woodland species, were chosen for the study because they represent two very different types of songbird. One of the findings was that during the autumn migration the purple martins stopped for three to four weeks in the Yucatan before continuing their journey to the Sao Paulo region in Brazil. Wood thrushes also broke their journey on their way to Honduras or Nicaragua.

By providing details on where the birds feed during their journey and where they spend the winter, the study should help identify areas that need to be protected to help conserve bird populations. Songbird populations have declined by thirty per cent around the world since the 1960s and accurate data on their requirements is vital to efforts to gauge the likely impacts of further habitat loss and climate change.

The purple martin, *Progne subis*

Silent Nights

Fears the neighbours will hear cries of passion are just as much a concern for chimpanzees as they are for people. Female chimpanzees make a conscious effort to keep the noise down when they are having sex so as to avoid alerting other animals to what is going on. While in humans the effort to keep quiet is often prompted by the potential for embarrassment, in chimpanzees it is to avoid a beating: higher-ranking females will attack any of a lower social standing that they catch mating.

After observing the animals in Uganda, researchers found that female chimps will stifle their "copulation calls" if they are aware of any other females within earshot, rather than risk provoking an attack and the break-up of any dalliance.

Chimpanzees are one of several creatures that cry out during sex – others include lions, elephants and brown rats – but their calls are thought to be less an expression of pleasure than a means of advertising themselves to other males. Female chimps can have sex up to 20 times a day, as they seek to mate with as many males as possible and the calls are thought by researchers to be a means of indicating availability and willingness.

Researchers from the University of St Andrews in the UK and the Max Planck Institute in Germany suggested that because both humans and chimps are aware of the possi-bility that they may be overheard during sex, a similar evolutionary mechanism may be involved.

New Species

We Meet at Last

In the age of instant communication it is often said that we live in a shrinking world, but it is still big enough for many species to remain hidden. Previously unknown animals and plants are still being described in their thousands each year. In 2007 alone there were 18,516 new species recorded according to The International Institute for Species Exploration. While few of the newly discovered animals approach even the size of a domestic cat – most could sit in a child's hand – they remain a source of fascination and often come in mesmerising colours or boast intriguing features. Most are found in the seas or in remote forests but they can still turn up in the most surprising places, like the tropical moth discovered in the centre of London.

Super Stick Insect

A jungle creepy crawly almost as long as a grown man's arm from shoulder to fingertip has been declared the world's longest insect. Chan's megastick, *Phobaeticus chani*, is a stick insect that lives in the jungle canopy and was discovered on the island of Borneo. It was found to measure 22.3in (56.7cm), making it 0.4in (1cm) longer than *P. serratipes*, a stick insect found in Malaysia and Indonesia which was previously held to be the longest in the world. Its body alone was 14.1in (35.7cm) long, making it 1.14in (2.9 cm) longer than the previous insect record holder for body length, another stick insect from Borneo, *P. Kirkyi*.

The creature's unique eggs were described by Dr Philip Bragg of the Phasmid Study Group – an organisation dedicated to the study of stick insects. The eggs, which the females are thought to flick into the air while in the canopy, are specially shaped to ensure that they float away from the parent insect by catching any available air current.

The insect measured 22.3in (56.7cm), almost as long as a grown man's arm from shoulder to fingertip

Researchers think that, like a variety of plant seeds, the eggs are designed to make use of breezes so that they hatch some distance away from the parent insects. This would have the advantages of reducing competition for food and mating between family members.

Dr Bragg was asked to look at the insect by Datuk Chan Chew Lun, an amateur naturalist from Malaysia for whom the insect was named and who suspected it was a new species when a farmer from Borneo gave it to him.

Once it had been analysed and described, the female stick insect, which resembles a dark green bamboo shoot, was donated to the Natural History Museum in the UK for display and further study. Only two others have been found and they are in collections in Sabah, the Malaysian region of Borneo where the insects were found. There are about 3,000 different species of stick insects in total; they mostly live in the tropics and sub-tropics and are most active at night.

Miniature Seahorses

Five new, tiny species of seahorse, including the smallest ever recorded, have been identified. The marine creatures are among the smallest vertebrates in the world and were described after being spotted by divers. All five live on reefs and have remained undiscovered for so long because of their diminutive size and a colouration that allows them to blend into the background. They are all classified as pygmy seahorses, which were first described scientifically in the 1970s. The new finds bring to nine the number of pygmy seahorses described by researchers.

The smallest of all the seahorses found was a specimen of Severns' seahorse, *Hippocampus severnsi*, which measured just 0.49in (12.4mm) from the tip of its snout to the tip of its tail. Little is known of its habits and preferences, but it has been seen in the waters of Indonesia, Japan, Papua New Guinea, the Solomon Islands and Fiji.

A second pygmy seahorse, described in a study by Dr Sara Lourie of McGill University in Canada and Rudie Kuiter of Museum Victoria in Australia, was named Satomi's seahorse, *H. satomiae*. Two specimens of Satomi's seahorse were slightly bigger than the smallest of the three Severns' seahorses collected, but they had a smaller average size. The average length of Satomi's seahorse was 0.54in (13.6mm) compared to 0.6in (15.2mm) for Severns' seahorse. Until their discovery the smallest seahorse was *H. denise*, which has an average length of 0.62in (15.7mm). The smallest of the species measured 0.52in (13.2mm) long.

Satomi's seahorses gather on small sea fans at night in groups of three to five and although they are coloured white and brown with red blotches, they give birth to jet black young.

Satomi's and Severns' seahorses were described at the same time as Pontoh's seahorse, *H. pontohi*, after being collected from Indonesian waters. All three were named after the divers who collected the specimens – Satomi Onishi, Mike Severns and Hense Pontoh. Shortly afterwards, early in 2009, two more pygmy seahorses were described by Dr Martin Gomon of Museum Victoria, and Rudie Kuiter. Like the other species, they had been seen on reefs by divers long before specimens could be collected for scientific analysis. The Walea seahorse, *H. waleananus*, also came from Indonesian waters, but the fifth seahorse, the soft-coral seahorse, *H. debelius*, came from the Red Sea. It was named after a marine naturalist, Helmut Debelius, who had spent more than a decade trying to find a specimen after it was first spotted in 1993.

Hippocampus satomiae attached to a coral

Death by Blooming

A palm tree that flowers itself to death in a single spectacular display was discovered during a family outing. Thousands of nectar-dripping flowers bloom on the tree, which expends so much of its reserves in creating the display that it dies of exhaustion immediately after producing seeds the size of grapes.

The Tahina palm, *Tahina spectabilis*, grows to more than 60ft (18m) tall but managed to escape notice until Xavier Metz, who manages a cashew plantation on Madagascar, took his family out for a walk. Mr Metz and his wife Nathalie stumbled on one of the flowering giants while walking and, never having seen anything quite like it, photographed it and posted the pictures on the internet when they reached home.

John Dransfield, co-author of *Field guide to the Palms of Madagascar*, was astonished when he saw the images, and when he saw samples he was certain that the tree was new to science. The discovery of the palm was announced in 2008 by researchers at the Royal Botanic Gardens, Kew, in the UK, who verified that the species was previously unknown.

Fewer than a hundred of the trees have been found on the island where they grow in just one small area of jungle in the north-west. The species has leaves up to 16ft (5m) in diameter, making them among the largest in the world for flowering plants. The tree is believed to grow for years before its single flowering and, unlike most of the palms on Madagascar, the Tahina species is on the much drier west side where temperatures average 27°C.

> The tree expends so much of its reserves blooming that it dies of exhaustion

When the flowering takes place so much nectar is exuded by the palm that insects, birds and other animals swarm over to make the most of the rich meal. It was named Tahina because the word means 'blessed' or 'protected' on Madagascar and is also named after Mr Metz's daughter, Anne-Tahina.

The palm the family found died before scientists could collect any of the seeds but a second tree was found flowering in September 2007. Botanists were able to return early in 2008 when the fruits had ripened. Enough seeds were collected to be sent for propagation and study to botanic gardens in several countries, including South Africa, Spain, Singapore, Australia, the US and the UK. Seeds have also been sent to the

UK's Millennium Seed Bank at the Royal Botanic Gardens, Wakehurst, where they are preserved in freezers alongside more than a billion other seeds from more than 20,000 species. The aim of the seed bank is to act as an ark for the seeds of every flowering plant in the world to protect them from extinction.

Hidden in Plain Sight

A Blue Starfish, *Linckia laevigata*, resting on hard Acropora coral.

Hundreds of animals that pass as background colour for tourists and professionals diving on reefs have been identified as unknown species. Soft corals, crustaceans and worms were among the species recorded for the first time in marine surveys off the Australian coast. They were found during expeditions off Lizard Island and Heron Island at the eastern end of the Great Barrier Reef system, and at Ningaloo Reef at the western end. Researchers were stunned by the number of species new to science that were recorded during the project because the Great Barrier Reef is so familiar to divers.

The research teams concentrated on less well-known types of animals such as worms and isopods and ignored larger and better-documented creatures such as fish and sea slugs. Of more than a thousand such creatures found during the expeditions, an estimated 300 to 500 had never been recorded before. New species included several basket stars, seaweeds and urchins, along with up to 100 worms, 130 crustaceans and 150 soft corals.

Isopods make up about three-quarters of the crustaceans thought to represent new species and are regarded as especially important because they are an indicator of the overall level of diversity. Many isopods feed on dead fish, which has earned them a reputation as the vultures of the sea, while others are parasitic. Cymothoids – a type of isopod located during the survey, though already known to be in the region – specialise in eating the tongues of live fish.

The surveys, led by the Australian Institute of Marine Science, were designed to help establish how many creatures live on corals, how many of them are found there exclusively, and how human interference affects them. The findings will form part of the worldwide Census of Marine Life.

The discovery of so many unknown species in one of the most explored marine zones was taken as an indicator of how little is known or understood of less accessible parts of the seas. Other creatures that provoked excitement among the research teams were unknown species of bristle worms – a marine relative of earthworms and leeches.

Live and Croaking

One of the smallest frogs in the world has been discovered after researchers followed the sound of croaking. The croaks of Nobel's pygmy frog could be heard long before scientists, with the assistance of local inhabitants, managed to pinpoint the source of the sounds in an area of scrub, grassland and cloud forest in Peru. They found the previously unrecorded frog hidden among the leaves and moss in an area known as the elfin forest. It proved to be the smallest amphibian in the Andes.

Though the frog, *Nobella pygmaea*, was small enough to sit comfortably on a fingernail, it turned out to be big on surprises. It is less than 0.45in (11.4mm) long and was found on mountainsides in the Manu National Park at elevations of 9,925 to 10,465ft (3,025 to 3,190m). The tiny size makes it one of the smallest vertebrates in the world to live above 9,900ft. The females lay just two eggs at a time, each of them 0.16in (4mm) in diameter; rather than abandoning them, the mothers remain close to the eggs to defend them from insect predators. Instead of being laid in water, as is the case with most amphibians, the eggs are laid in moist leaf litter or moss. Furthermore, the eggs hatch immediately into juvenile frogs, skipping the tadpole stage.

A team of German and Peruvian herpetologists discovered the frog and are confident its diminutive size confers some advantage to the species, but they have yet to find out what it is. Dr Edgar Lehr of the Senckenberg Natural History Collection in Dresden, Germany, and Dr Alessandro Catenazzi of the University of California, Berkeley, in the US studied the frog and are confident there are plenty more unknown species waiting to be discovered in the Andes.

above: **Nobel's pygmy frog,** *Nobella pygmaea*
below: **The frog's habitat, the cloud forest of Peru**

Shocking Pink Poison

A shocking pink millipede which oozes cyanide has been found in an Asian rainforest region. It was one of more than a thousand previously unknown species of animal or plant that have turned up at the rate of two a week in this wildlife hotspot. The Greater Mekong, a little explored region of South-East Asia, which extends over six countries, is proving to be a Lost World of wildlife treasures.

Among the most eye-catching of the discoveries, researchers saw the bright pink dragon millipede for the first time in 2007 when they encountered several of them clambering over limestone rocks and on palm leaves. It is thought that the bright colouration is a warning to other animals that the millipedes are dangerous and best avoided – swallowing them is likely to be fatal despite the animal being only 1.2in. (3cm) long. The millipede, *Desmoxytes purpurosea*, is one of more than two dozen dragon millipedes in South-East Asia. It produces cyanide in glands that give it the characteristic almond smell associated with the poison beloved by crime writers.

The millipede was discovered by Professor Henrik Enghoff of the Natural History Museum of Denmark at the University of Copenhagen, and Somsak Panha of Chulalongkorn University in Thailand. They had heard rumours of the existence of a reddish millipede and launched an expedition to Thailand. They found the brightly coloured invertebrate almost as soon as they reached the Hup Pa Tard mountain. The researchers were so struck by the colouration that they felt it deserved more than just a Latin name so dubbed it the "shocking pink dragon millipede".

During ten years of surveys and exploration of the Greater Mekong (1997-2007), 1068 new species of animals and plants were identified by researchers, and there are several thousand more unknown invertebrates still to be fully catalogued. According to the World Wildlife Fund finds include 519 new species of plants, 89 frogs, 279 fish, 22 snakes, 46 lizards, four turtles, two salamanders and 15 mammals.

A cave-dwelling spider bigger than a dinner plate was among the 88 new species of spider discovered in the ten-year period. With a leg-span of 12in (30cm) *Heteropoda maxima* is the biggest huntsman spider in the world, but despite its ferocious countenance it is thought to limit its prey to large insects. Little is known about its behaviour but it is fast on its feet and has a venomous bite, although it is not regarded as dangerous to humans.

Discoveries in the Greater Mekong are still being made and the region is regarded as so rich in unknown animals and plants that it has been compared to those parts of the world where rich finds were made in previous centuries. China, Thailand, Burma, Laos, Vietnam and Cambodia all have territory in the rainforest and wetland region on either side of

> The millipede produces cyanide in glands, giving it the characteristic almond smell associated with the poison

a 2,800 mile (4,500km) stretch of the Mekong River. The river basin itself is richer than the Amazon in wildlife species per mile and is home to the rare Irrawaddy dolphin and the Mekong catfish, one of the largest freshwater fish in the world. At least 1,300 species of fish live there and new ones are still being counted.

One of the biggest surprises for scientists trying to survey the wildlife in the region was the discovery of the Laotian rock rat, *Laonastes aenigmamus*. Researchers first found the rock rat for sale in a market in Laos in 1996. The locals regarded it as food and knew it as the *kha-nyou*. It was described as a new species in 2005, but it was not until the following year that scientists were able to find and photograph a live specimen for the first time, when David Redfield, professor emeritus at Florida State University and Uthai Treesucon, a biologist from Thailand, caught one in the village of Doy. Initially the rock rat, which walks like a duck, was thought to be from an entirely new family of mammals, but in 2006 it was identified as the last surviving member of a group of rodents that was thought to have become extinct eleven million years ago.

Another discovery was first spotted in a restaurant. The pit viper, *Trimeresurus vogeli*, was identified as a new species in 2001 after being spotted slithering through the rafters of a restaurant in the Khao Yai National Park in Thailand. Other new species discovered in the Greater Mekong include the Annamite striped rabbit, *Nesolagus timminsi*, one of only two types of striped rabbit known to researchers, and two types of muntjac deer – *Muntiacus truongsonensis* in Vietnam in 1998 and *Muntiacus putaoensis* in Burma a year later, as well as a woolly bat, *Kerivoula titania*, in Cambodia in 2007.

Out of the Depths

A previously unknown carnivorous sea squirt living in pitch blackness has been found in a trench at depths no human diver could survive. Unlike most of its relatives, the sea squirt has eschewed a diet of plankton and other microscopic meals in favour of larger prey. Instead of pumping seawater through its body and filtering out tiny morsels of food, it waits in the darkness for a shrimp or fish to bump into it. When triggered by contact the sea squirt's funnel-like body collapses onto its prey and envelops it.

The 20in (50cm) long sea squirt was found living as deep as 13,143ft (4,006m) under the waves in the Tasman Fracture Zone off the south-west coast of Australia. It was spotted by scientists using a remote-operated submersible called Jason, and its discovery made it the deepest-living creature in Australian waters. The previously unseen squirt lives in the trench, which is a crack in the earth's crust more than 2.5 miles (4km) deep.

The trench had previously only been explored to a depth of 5,900ft (1,800m) and scientists wanted to find out what else might lurk at lower depths. Other new species of marine creature discovered by Australian and US researchers during the expedition included a type of barnacle, a sea anemone that mimics coral, and a bright red species of Gorgon's Head coral. As well as discovering new species, the submersible revealed patches of seabed heaving with deep sea life.

Dr Jess Adkins of the California Institute of Technology described one seamount he saw as so full of orange spider crabs and purple corals that it looked "like a bouquet". Other structures were equally colourful and he said it was like viewing "English gardens" beneath the sea as the submersible sailed over them. Dr Ron Thresher of Australia's Climate Adaptation and Wealth from Oceans project said that the ecosystem deep within the trench was dominated by gooseneck barnacles and purple-spotted sea anemones. Expedition members using Jason, which is owned and operated by the Wood Hole Oceanographic Institution in the US, found extensive fields of fossilised corals at depths of more than 4,600ft (1,400m). They were dated to more than 10,000 years old and are expected to yield data on past climates.

> The submersible revealed patches of the sea bed teeming with unknown life

The ecosystem within the trench is dominated by gooseneck barnacles (left) and purple sea anemones (overleaf)

Orchid Hotspot

Orchid hunters are enjoying a golden age of discovery. They have uncovered more than 1,500 new species in less than a decade. The rate at which the plants have been found has been unmatched for decades and no more so than in Ecuador where the construction of new roads has allowed access to some of the world's most remote and unspoilt forests leading to the discovery of more than a thousand new orchids since the turn of the century.

Among the most spectacular finds was a group of 28 closely related orchids which had evolved in a mountainous area the size of London. They were from the teagueia genus, which was thought to be restricted to just six species of orchid across the world. The evolution of the 28 closely related orchids has been described as a botanical version of Darwin's finches.

Dr Lou Jost, a botanist with the EcoMinga Foundation, is one of the world's leading orchid hunters with sixty new species to his name, along with ten other types of plant. He named one of the plants, a tree with a "blousy, flashy" bright blue flower, after Sir David Attenborough, the naturalist and the patron of the World Land Trust in the UK, which partnered EcoMinga in conservation projects in Ecuador. It was called *Blakea attenboroughii*. Dr Jost reckons on finding each year five to ten species of orchid that have never been described before, often in regions of forest never before visited by humans. "It's a very exciting feeling to find a new species. People think everything has been discovered but there's much more to be discovered," he said.

The diversity of Ecuador's forests is so rich and wide ranging that several new species can be found on a single mountain. Across South America there are 90-100,000 species of flowering plants, more than double the number found in the African and Asian tropics combined. Part of the reason South America boasts more species than any other continent is the huge variation in terrain in the Andes regions and the weather patterns they experience. In one part of Ecuador the change is so extreme that the wettest and driest parts of the country lie within 40 miles of each other. Scientists remain uncertain, however, why quite so many species of plants have evolved so close together.

> A group of 28 closely related orchids had evolved in an area the size of London

A collection of recently discovered orchids of the genus teagueia

The Smallest Snake in the World

A newly discovered snake with a girth comparable to a strand of spaghetti has been named the world's smallest. At just four inches (10cm) long and about 0.08 inches (2mm) in diameter the Barbados threadsnake, *Leptotyphlops carlae*, is tiny enough to be dwarfed by many earthworms. While some snakes are big enough to tackle animals the size of deer, the Barbados threadsnake has to limit its ambition to smaller prey – mainly ants, termites and their larvae. It is 0.16 inches (4mm) smaller than the Martinique threadsnake, *L. bilineatus*, which was previously regarded as the smallest of more than 3,100 species of snake around the world. Despite its size and lack of poison to help subdue prey, the snake has been described as a voracious hunter.

The Barbados species is one of about 300 types of threadsnake and as such was described as "the smallest of the smallest" by Professor Blair Hedges of the Pennsylvania State University in the United States, who discovered it. Professor Hedges came across the snake as he inspected stones, rotten logs and other potential hiding places amidst the undergrowth during a survey of snakes, lizards and amphibians on the Caribbean island of Barbados. So small is the species that the females have to devote fifteen per cent of their body-length to the eggs, a bigger proportion than any other snake, and can only develop and lay one at a time.

> **Despite its size the snake is a voracious hunter of ants and termites**

When they hatch, the infant snakes are half the size of the adult – the equivalent of a human mother giving birth to a 60lb baby. Professor Hedges, who named the new discovery after his wife Carla Ann Hass, said that when compared to the mother's body, the size of the egg suggests that there is a critical size for the young snakes below which they are unlikely to survive. The minimum size, he suggested, is likely to be determined by the availability of prey small enough to be caught and eaten by the young.

At the same time as announcing the existence of the Barbados threadsnake he reported the discovery of another species new to science – the St Lucia threadsnake, *L. breuili*. Professor Hedges is also responsible for the discovery of the world's smallest frog, *Eleutherodactylus iberia*, and the tiniest lizard, *Sphaerodactylus ariasae*. He dismissed his record for finding the three smallest creatures of their species as "just coincidence".

Stalking Spiders

Up to fifty new species of spider, each capable of jumping thirty times their own body length, have been found in tropical undergrowth. The jumping spiders were among the highlights of a month-long expedition to a little-explored region of Papua New Guinea. Three of the spiders were so different from any known to science that researchers concluded they came from evolutionary branches never before encountered.

More than 600 types of animal were recorded overall during the Rapid Assessment Programme led by Conservation International.

Professor Wayne Maddison of the University of British Columbia in Canada was one of the researchers who took part in the expedition to the Kaijende highlands and the Hewa wilderness and was delighted to find unknown jumping spiders. They were, he enthused, "so cute".

The finds were so numerous and diverse that they are expected to offer new insights into how and why it was that they evolved after other types of spider, which rely on silken threads to catch prey.

Jumping spiders, instead of waiting for prey to come to them, seek out their meals and will stalk and pounce on a variety of insects. Their sight is so well evolved that they are able to distinguish between the motions of different types of prey and can vary their attack technique according to the species they are trying to catch

The thirty to fifty new species of jumping spiders – the final number depends on laboratory analysis – were just some of the finds during the 2008 summer expedition. Other wildlife found in the haul of new species included three frogs, two plants, a gecko, several beetles and some web-building spiders.

Moreover, he said, the finds could help bring about advances in medical science because study of the venoms may reveal chemicals that can form the basis of new drugs.

Similarly, the eyes could help in the development of robotic vision. In humans and other animals the retina is hemispherical, but jumping spiders have a miniaturised, flat scanning retina which flicks from side to side to form a single picture by putting together several horizontal images. The flat retina is found in two of the invertebrates' eight eyes and they offer the animal high resolution images that ensure it has better vision than web-building spiders. Jumping spiders have, in effect, deconstructed the eyeball and rebuilt it in miniature, section by section, with modifications that could inspire robot designers.

Some of the great diversity of body forms and colours found in salticids from Papua New Guinea.

Blue Bones and Green Blood

A frog with green blood and turquoise bones has been discovered as part of a project to rebuild Cambodia's scientific community from the ashes left by the rule of the Khmer Rouge. The Samkos bush frog was uncovered in a remote area of the Cardamom Mountains that was once a stronghold of the regime that killed an estimated 1.5 million people and destroyed many of the country's institutions. The startling colour of the frog's blood and bones are caused by the pigment biliverdin. In other animals the pigment is a waste product that would be processed in the liver but in the Samkos bush frog, *Chriomantis samkosensis*, it is put into the blood stream. The pigment, which appears green

> The green colour of the frog's blood and bones is caused by the pigment biliverdin

through the amphibian's translucent skin, helps camouflage the frog and makes it particularly hard to spot in its jungle habitat. Researchers trying to photograph it were usually only able to pinpoint its position by listening to its distinctive rising trill calls.

The frog was discovered by Jeremy Holden, a naturalist for Fauna & Flora International (FFI), who was thrilled by the discovery of a species new to science. The researchers think that it probably breeds in temporary jungle pools filled by heavy rain and that the unusual hue of its blood may act as a warning to potential predators that the animal has a nasty taste.

The Samkos bush frog was one of four new species discovered during FFI conservation surveys of the Cardamom Mountains over the eight years since 2000. The other three were Smith's frog, *Rana faber*, the Aural horned frog, *Megophrys auralensis*, and the Cardamom bush frog, *Philautus cardamomus*. No work to study the wildlife in much of the region could be done for many years because it was a Khmer Rouge strong-hold from the early 1970s until 1998. Many scientists, as part of the educated intelligentsia, were killed while the Khmer Rouge was in power, but attempts are now being made to train a new generation.

Zoology and botany are among the fields being re-established, and

opposite: **The Samkos bush frog**
right: **The Cardamom bush frog**

alongside its survey work the FFI has helped to promote training. It also played a role in setting up the *Cambodian Journal of Natural History* and the country's first natural history museum.

Many of the plants and animals in Cambodia, especially those in the more remote regions, are little known but survey work is slowly uncovering them. Conservationists exploring the Cardamom Mountains not only discovered four previously unseen species of frog, but found more than forty species of amphibians that, while known to science, had never been recorded before in Cambodia. According to naturalists the region's biodiversity is so rich and diverse that it is one of Asia's wildlife jewels. The researchers are therefore confident that plenty more unknown species await discovery.

right: **Smith's frog**
below: **The Aural horned frog**

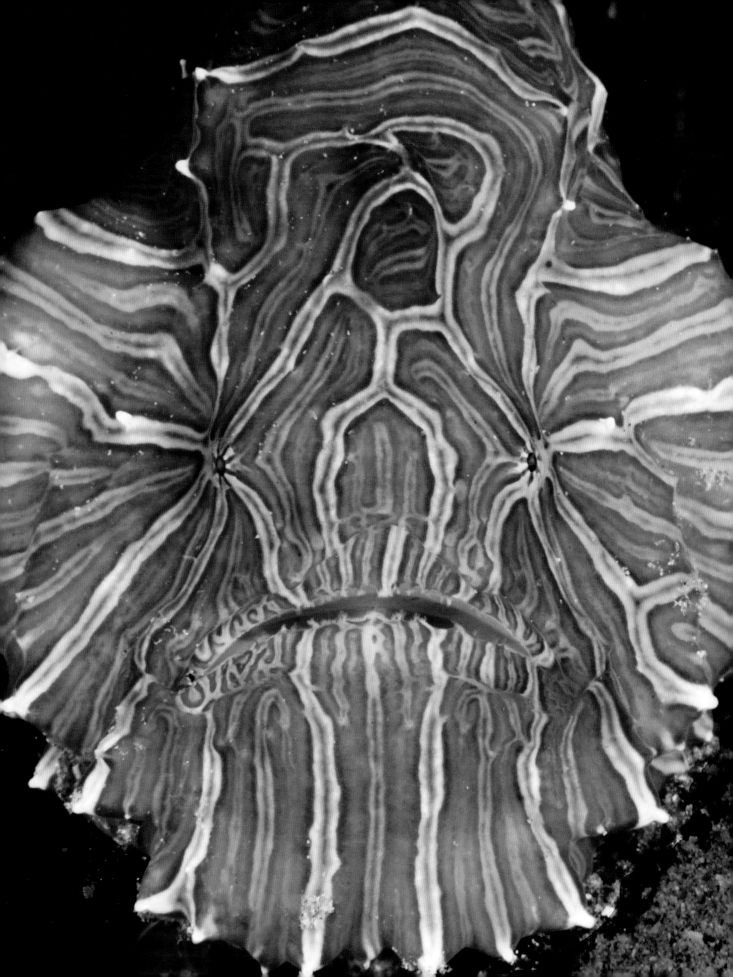

Rubber Ball Fish

A jet-propelled fish that prefers bouncing to swimming has been named as a new species after being photographed by divers. The brightly-coloured fish bounces around reefs on the Indonesian coast by pushing itself off the seabed with its fins while expelling water from its gills in a form of jet propulsion. It is a type of frogfish, but unlike others that use their jet propulsion to lift them upwards before swimming forwards, the newly discovered species prefers to hop about. Rather than bouncing forward in a predictable fashion, its movement is chaotic, and researchers have described its motion as akin to a drunken rubber ball. The frogfish has thick folds of skin to prevent it from being damaged by sharp corals, and was named *Histiophryne psychedelica* to reflect the wild colouration of white swirling stripes on a peach or yellow-brown background.

It was identified as a frogfish, which are themselves a type of anglerfish, after being seen in 2008 by divers Toby Fadirsyair and Buck and Fitrie Randolph in an area of Ambon Harbour known as "the twilight zone" because of the number of rare animals. None of them had seen anything quite like it, so they sent photographs to Professor Ted Pietsch of the University of Washington in the US, who led the research to identify it. Samples of DNA were taken, which helped to establish it as a previously unrecog-nised species, but Professor Pietsch knew he was dealing with an unusual creature the moment he saw it.

One of its oddest features are the forward-facing eyes in its broad, flat face – fish usually have eyes on the sides of their heads. This suggests that *Histiophryne psychedelica* may have binocular vision. Observations have shown that the fish particularly likes finding nooks and crevices in the coral which it can squeeze into. Researchers watched several times as the fish painstakingly pushed their way into small cavities where they would be safe from predators. It may well be that the fish, having blocked any escape by squeezing into the cavities, may have cornered prey inside.

Researchers studying the bouncing frogfish found that its bright colours quickly vanished when it was preserved in ethanol and it appeared white, although the pattern of stripes remained visible under the microscope. In 1992 Professor Pietsch had been sent two specimens of faded fish but had dismissed them as another type of frogfish, *H. cryptacanthus*. The discovery of *H. psychedelica* prompted him to look again. Both specimens had been retained in the University of Washington's fish collection and once the distinctive swirling stripes had been revealed under the microscope, they were reclassified as the psychedelic frogfish. They had originally been found in a shipment of live fish from Bali in Indonesia sent to the Dallas Aquarium in the US, where they were dubbed "Paisley frogfish" because of their unusual pigmentation. The two fish arrived at the aquarium "in very poor condition" and died soon afterwards. Photographs were of poor quality and when the preserved remains were sent to Professor Pietsch they had faded so he gave them only a cursory examination.

> The frogfish's movement is chaotic, like a drunken rubber ball

Caught on Camera!

The biggest elephant-shrew in the world managed to keep its existence a secret until it wandered into the view-finder of a camera-trap set up in a remote mountain forest. The motion-sensing camera had been set up to record a forest antelope, but one of the exposures revealed the fuzzy outline of a mysterious mammal. Further camera traps were put in place, and researchers succeeded in identifying the creature as a new species of elephant-shrew.

An expedition to the Udzungwa mountains of Tanzania was mounted to find live specimens, and after enduring non-stop rain for several days, researchers managed to catch one. The animal was not just a previously unknown species but one that dwarfed all the rest of the known species. At 22in (56cm) long and weighing in at an average of 1lb 9oz (710g) the grey-faced giant elephant-shrew, *Rhynchocyon udzungwensis*, is up to 20 per cent longer and 50 per cent heavier than any other. It was so much bigger than it appeared in the photographs that all the traps the expedition members had used to try to catch it proved too small to be of any use, and the team had to resort to snares.

Dr Galen Rathbun of the California Academy of Sciences has spent so much of his career studying elephant-shrews that he is known as "the elephant-shrew guy", but even he was astonished at the size of the new species. When the first of four of the animals was captured it was carried off triumphantly in a pillow case to Dr Rathbun as he sheltered in his tent from the rain. He initially dismissed any thought of it being an elephant-shrew when he took the animal from a colleague, still wrapped up, because it felt so heavy. It was only when he peered inside the pillow case and saw the unmistakeable long snout did he realise that it really was an elephant-shrew – one with a black bottom, russet-orange flanks and a pale cream chest and chin. Researchers estimate that there are something like 15,000 to 24,000 of the newly discovered species scampering around a mountain forest region of Tanzania that covers 116 sq.miles (300sq.km). The creatures sleep in nests, and most of them live above altitudes of 3,280ft (1,000m). All are found in Africa.

Elephant-shrews, which scientists today prefer to call sengis, get their name from their distinctive snout, which is long and flexible and bears comparison with an elephant's trunk. When they were first studied in detail by Western scientists in the mid-nineteenth century, they were thought to be close relations of shrews, hedgehogs and moles. In recent years, however, scientists have realised that they have no close relations but that their nearest kin include elephants, aardvarks and sea cows. Insects probably comprise the bulk, if not the entirety of their diet; they find them by poking their snouts into leaves and other debris lying on the floor of their high altitude forest habitat. Once an insect is detected the giant elephant-shrew shoots out its tongue and flicks its prey into its mouth.

Their nearest kin include elephants, aardvarks and sea cows

The grey-faced sengi was the first elephant-shrew to be discovered for more than 125 years but another, the seventeenth, was identified just a few months later. Karoo rock elephant-shrews, *Elephantulus pilicaudus*, had been held in museum collections for more than thirty years but no one had realised that they were distinct from Cape rock elephant-shrews, *E. edwardii*. When researchers from Stellenbosch University in South Africa started analysing the genetic differences between what they thought were the Cape rock elephant-shrews, they began to suspect there was enough variation to justify the naming of a new species. Their suspicions were confirmed when more of the animals were captured in the wild and studied. While the Cape rock and Karoo rock species look virtually the same, there are slight differences apparent to expert eyes in their tail shapes and the colour of their flanks. Karoo rock elephant-shrews are another high altitude species, found above 4,265ft (1,300m). They are found in South Africa where they are confined to the Western Cape and Northern Cape.

The Lost Forest

A mountain forest little known even in its home country is beginning to yield up its secrets after being discovered through Google Earth. Scientists at the UK's Royal Botanic Gardens, Kew, were experimenting with the Google Earth system in 2005 to try and identify forest regions that should be conserved when they stumbled across a vast untouched area.

Investigations quickly established that knowledge of the existence of the 31 sq.miles (80 sq.km) of pristine forest on Mount Mabu in Mozambique was limited almost exclusively to villagers who lived in the region. The country was racked by civil war from the 1970s to 1992, leaving up to a million people dead, and villagers kept quiet about the forest because it provided them with a valuable refuge while roads and buildings outside it were being destroyed.

A team of researchers from Mozambique, Tanzania, Malawi, Switzerland, Belgium and the UK travelled to the forest to carry out a preliminary exploration in October and November 2008 and were awed by the diversity of wildlife that they found. Three species of butterflies that had never been described before were discovered, and researchers are confident many more unknown species await them in the forest. Six suspected new species of reptiles, including a forest adder, have already been found, as have new populations of seven species of bird that are threatened worldwide with extinction.

More than 500 plant specimens were brought out of the forest, and among the animals the researchers saw were pygmy chameleons, Swynnerton's robin, gaboon vipers, the emperor swallowtail butterfly, and the small striped swordtail butterfly.

According to Jonathan Timberlake, a Kew botanist and leader of the expedition, the forest is thought to be the biggest medium altitude forest area in southern Africa, yet it had gone unnoticed. He described the diversity of the plants and animals in the forest, including rarely seen orchids, klipspringer and blue duiker antelopes, samango monkeys and elephant shrews – as "mind-boggling".

> Knowledge of the forest was limited almost exclusively to villagers in that region

left clockwise: **Olive sunbird, Atheris snake, hemipteran bug, common leopard butterflies, pygmy chameleon**

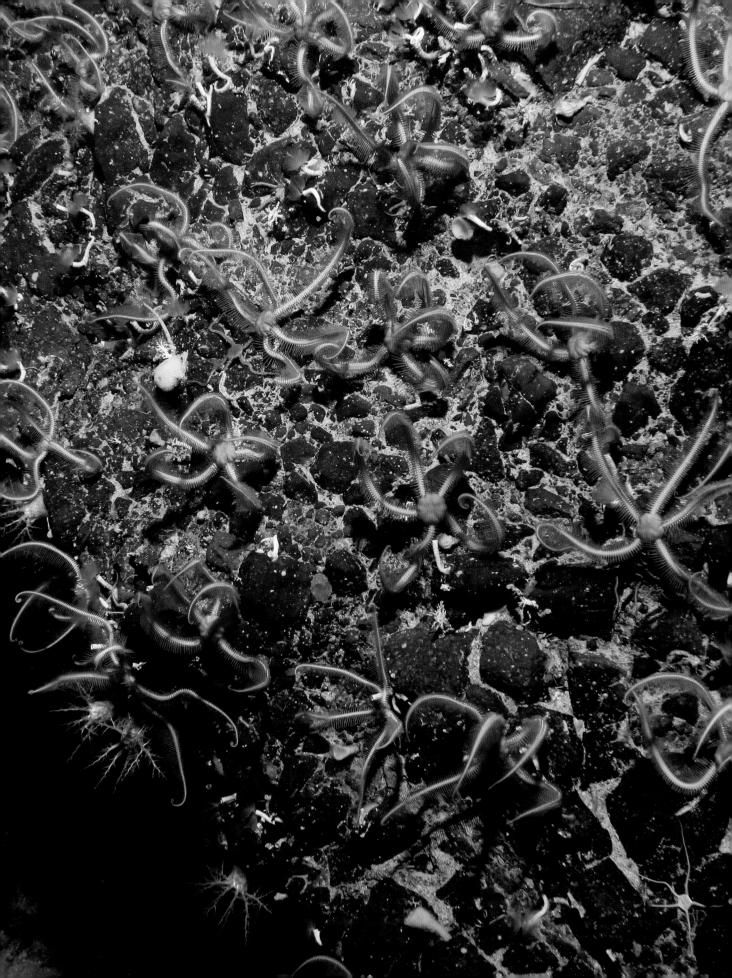

Brittle-star City

Tens of millions of brittle-stars have been found in what represents a unique and previously unseen marine habitat. The brittle-stars, a relation of starfish and sea urchins, covered the summit of a seamount which formed part of an under-water range of mountains and rose 2,500ft (750m) from the seabed. They were the only creatures visible on the flat surface of the seamount and are thought to be the only inhabitants because no other animals in the area are strong enough to hold on.

The seamount, a marine mountain that is not high enough to break the surface of the sea, is swept by the Antarctic Circumpolar Current, making it difficult for anything to cling on to the rock. An estimated 35 million cu.ft (one million cu.m) flow every second through a 50-mile stretch of the Macquarie Ridge, a line of underwater mountains running southwards from New Zealand for 870 miles (1,400 km). Water rushes over the rock at 2.3mph (3.7kph) but the five-armed brittle-stars manage to cling on and to find enough food to live on by snatching fragments of organic matter from the current.

Corals and sponges usually dominate the tops of seamounts. The discovery of the brittle-stars on the Macquarie Ridge is the first where they are the predominant (and in this case exclusive) creature. They were packed so densely that there were several hundred in a square yard.

The brittle-stars found on the summit of the seamount were types that had previously been recorded in other parts of the world, but at least one species new to science was seen on another part of the underwater mountain. Nine previously unknown species of starfish and sponges (subject to verification) were also discovered during the expedition. Another surprise for the scientists was the discovery of large numbers of deep-water cardinal fish seen sheltering below a rock ledge. It is probably by sheltering from the full force of the current in crevices and making darting forays into the fast-flowing water to snatch morsels of food that they can conserve enough energy to survive on the seamount.

Exploration of the ridge was carried out as a joint project between New Zealand and Australian research institutions, including the Commonwealth Scientific and Industrial Research Organisation, Museum Victoria, and the National Institute of Water & Atmospheric Research. Special marine sleds towed by a research vessel were used to collect samples but much of the survey was conducted using a towed submersible carrying cameras.

Tens of thousands of seamounts are hidden beneath the surface of the oceans but only a few hundred have been explored in any detail. The seamount that hosted the brittle-star community, dubbed Brittle-star City by the research team, peaked 295ft (90m) beneath the surface of the ocean and had a flat top, thought to have been created by erosion some 18,000 years ago during the last Ice Age when sea levels were much lower than they are today.

> The brittle-stars cling on and find enough food by snatching fragments of organic matter from the current

Climate Change
Too Hot to Handle

Climate change and global warming are terms which over the last twenty years have forced their way first into public consciousness and then into common parlance. The majority of the scientific community now agree that temperatures are rising worldwide as a direct result of mankind's activities. In particular, the use of fossil fuels is a cause for concern. The worst of the potential impacts – such as the possibility that much of southern Europe will become an uninhabitable wasteland because of the intense heat – have yet to be seen, but some are beginning to show themselves. It is already possible to detect shifts in the populations of animals and plants as they try to move away from habitats that are becoming too hot for them. As the century progresses, many more species are likely to be driven out of their traditional territories as they seek refuge further north or higher up mountains.

Penguin Marathons

Penguins at one of the world's largest colonies are being forced to commute up to 25 extra miles to find food compared to the distance they swam just a decade ago. The fish and squid that the penguins eat are increasingly being found further north, meaning that the aquatic birds have to travel further to reach them. Changes in the ocean currents driven by climate change are thought to be one of the factors influencing where the fish can be found.

Magellanic penguins at the Punta Tombo colony on the Argentine coast are being forced to swim up to 25 miles (40km) further to reach their food and then another 25 extra miles back again. The distances can make the difference between the penguins being able to raise their chicks successfully or seeing their offspring starve. On average they have to commute 37 miles (60km) more than in the 1990s.

Professor Dee Boersma of the University of Washington in the US has been studying penguins at the colony since 1982 and said the distance penguins have to travel to forage is crucial. When they have to swim 93 miles (150km) or less to get adequate stocks of food for their young they have a high probability of raising chicks successfully during the breeding season, but when they have to swim more than 217 miles (350km), there is virtually no chance of rearing the chicks.

During the breeding season a foraging Magellanic penguin has to catch enough fish to feed its chicks – two eggs are generally laid – and to provide a meal for its partner, who stays behind to babysit. A foraging parent can be away for two weeks in search of food, but the longer the chicks go hungry the less chance they have of surviving. A further factor mitigating against Magellanic penguins raising their chicks successfully is the fact that they are laying their eggs six days later than they did two decades ago, giving their young less time to fatten up before they have to fend for themselves.

Professor Boersma said that the penguins at Punta Tombo – the biggest Magellanic colony in the world – appear to have been dealt a second blow by the effects of climate change. Weather patterns have altered, causing more heavy rain to fall during the breeding season. Magellanic penguins, which can live for more than thirty years, nest in burrows, and when rainfall levels rise there is an increased risk of flooding, which can drown the chicks or leave them so wet that they suffer from exposure.

More than a million pairs of Magellanic penguins, *Spheniscus magellanicus*, from colonies on the southern coasts of Argentina and Chile and on the Falkland Islands are estimated to be alive today, but the number is falling. At Punta Tombo the numbers have fallen from more than 350,000 pairs in the 1970s to 200,000 in 2006. Climate change is blamed as one factor in the decline but there are other problems faced by the penguins, such as oil pollution and overfishing. Nor is the Magellanic penguin the only species in difficulty. Professor Boersma, the director of the Wildlife Conservation Society's Penguin Project, said that twelve of the seventeen penguin species are declining fast.

> The distances can make the difference between the penguins being able to raise their chicks or seeing them starve

Killer Heat Waves

Flying foxes have been dropping from trees in their thousands as extreme temperatures take their toll on the animals. Temperature rises, thought to be linked to climate change, have been devastating for the fruit bats, which are exposed to the sun as they sleep hanging from trees in the daytime. It is estimated that more than 30,000 have been killed by the heat in less than fifteen years as a series of heat waves have swept Australia. Mass mortality among flying foxes, which can have wingspans of 5ft (1.5m), has taken place at least nineteen times since 1994 because of extreme heat. Previously there were just three anecdotal reports of such deaths. The flying fox is the largest mammal, apart from humans, that has demonstrably suffered mass mortality in a heat wave.

Flying foxes were observed making desperate efforts to cool themselves down when temperatures approached and rose above 42°C in New South Wales, Australia, on 12 January, 2002. They fanned themselves with their wings, they panted, they sought what shade they could find and, as a last resort, they rubbed saliva on their skin to replace lost water but of the 26,500 to 30,800 estimated to be living in one mixed species colony, at least 1,453 were killed by the heat. Temperatures endured by the animals were several degrees hotter than the 35.3°C average maximum temperature for the summer months.

Members of a research team led by Dr Justin Welbergen of the University of Cambridge in the UK observed the effects of the extreme temperatures on the flying foxes as they unfurled at the roost at Dallis Park on the east coast of Australia. Flying foxes at the colony showed the first signs of discomfort at 10am, when they began wing-fanning, and by the early afternoon they began to drop from the tree canopies where they were roosting. Once the bats had fallen from their roosts they survived for only another ten to twenty minutes, and the first deaths took place about an hour before temperatures at the nearest weather station recorded an all-time high of 42.9°C. Temperatures had previously reached 41.2°C in 1994 at the same weather station without any heat-related deaths being observed at the Dallis Park bat colony.

Two species of fruit bat sharing the colony suffered fatalities during the January 12 heat wave. The worst affected, proportionate to its population size, was the black flying fox, which accounted for 92 per cent of the deaths at Dallis Park, with the rest being grey-headed flying foxes. Researchers calculated that 10 to 13 per cent of black flying foxes, *Pteropus alecto*, at the Dallis Park colony were killed by the heat, and that juveniles were the most vulnerable.

Mass deaths were recorded among grey-headed and black flying foxes in nine bat colonies in the Northern Rivers area, which stretches 155 miles (250km) along the east coast and covers 4,250 sq.miles (11,000 sq.km). A third species, the little red flying fox, *Pteropus scapulatus*, appeared to be

Mass deaths were recorded among grey-headed and black flying foxes

unaffected. All nine of the colonies experienced maximum temperatures ranging from 41.7°C to 43.4°C and at least 3,679 flying foxes are known to have died, although researchers think that this figure is an underestimate.

Grey-headed flying foxes, *Pteropus poliocephalus*, suffered the greatest number of fatalities in the 19 mass mortalities reported from 1994 to 2007 in New South Wales, Queensland and Victoria. It is thought that they accounted for 24,500 of the more than 30,000 deaths. The effect of heat is a further conservation concern for the grey-headed flying fox, which was once counted in millions but is now down to 400,000 individuals worldwide after suffering a 30 per cent decline in numbers from 1989 to 2001.

The research team, which included scientists from the universities of Queensland and New England in Australia, and the University of Ulm in Germany, described climate change as "a double-edged sword" for the black flying fox. Although it is vulnerable to extreme heat, it has still been able to expand its range 465 miles (750km) southwards in Australia since 1928 because of a reduction in the incidence of night frosts, which it cannot tolerate. Both species of flying fox forage at night for fruit, pollen and nectar and are regarded as important pollinators of both wild and cultivated plants.

Climate change is "a double-edged sword" for the black flying fox

Egg Timers

Great tits are the first animal shown to respond flexibly to climate change – but not all of them can do it. To the surprise of researchers, two separate populations of the bird reacted differently to the challenge presented by rising temperatures. A group of the birds being monitored in the United Kingdom has been able to alter the time they lay their eggs to fit in with warming conditions. But birds of the same species in the Netherlands, have not demonstrated the same adaptability needed to cope with the climatic changes blamed on global warming.

Tits have had to be flexible because of changes in the timing of the arrival of spring. Many spring events, such as the movements of migratory birds, the first buds to grow on trees, and the appearance of insects, take place earlier in the year than they did fifty years ago. Warmer temperatures caused by man-made climate change have been widely attributed as the cause. The shifts can be by as little as a day or well over a month, depending on the species involved and the region of the world.

Great tits, *Parus major*, in the UK have responded by laying their eggs two weeks earlier on average than they did in the 1950s. It is thought the shift began in the 1970s. They also react to whether the spring is warmer, colder or much the same as it was the previous year rather than simply shifting to ever earlier egg-laying dates. They are the first animals to demonstrate an ability to track the fluctuations in temperature from year to year so that in warmer springs they can start their families earlier than in the colder years.

The ability of the birds – monitored in Wytham Woods near Oxford – to vary their laying dates means that they can time the birth of their chicks to the time when the insects they depend on for food become available. Each pair of great tits raise an average of eight chicks per nest, and sometimes as many as fifteen, and the parents have to catch about five hundred insects – especially caterpillars – a day to feed them.

Researchers at the universities of Oxford and Edinburgh in the UK found that the date that the tits laid their eggs was linked to the availability of winter moth caterpillars, *Operophtera brumata*, which form a significant part of the chicks' diet. By responding to the temperatures experienced before they start laying their eggs the parent birds make sure the winter moth caterpillars are available by the time their chicks hatch.

By contrast, an earlier study indicated that great tits in the Netherlands showed a much weaker response to changes in temperature. Those changes that were observed in the Netherlands were thought to be driven primarily by the 'survival of the fittest' factor – those that bred too early or too late stood a much lower chance of successfully raising chicks. Those that laid eggs at the right time for the caterpillars did so out of serendipity rather than as a response to temperature changes. Professor Ben Sheldon of the University of Oxford said that he would have expected the two great tit populations to react in the same way, and that it was a mystery why they responded differently to climate change.

opposite: **Female great tit incubating in nest**
below: **Great tit hatchling**

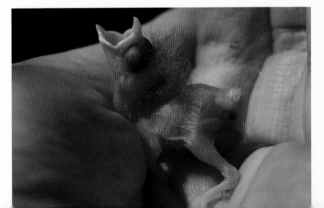

Tough at the Top

Hotter conditions in the tropics since the mid-1960s have driven moths up mountains in search of cooler weather. Observations of moths on Mount Kinabalu in Borneo have revealed that over a 42-year period they shifted upwards by an average of 220ft (67m). The discovery is the first to demonstrate the changes wrought on insect populations in the tropics by global warming and it is thought likely that the shift will be repeated in mountainous regions around the world.

The study, led by researchers from the University of York in the United Kingdom, was made possible because, in 1965, long before the possibility of global warming had been raised, a group of scientists explored Mount Kinabalu and made a comprehensive record of all they found as they progressed. Among the notes were details of all the species of moths that they had found, together with the heights at which they were seen. These records, together with photographs of the sites at which they worked, meant that in 2007 another scientific team was able to follow in their footsteps. The 2007 expedition included Henry Barlow, one of the members of the original party.

During the survey the researchers managed to trap 102 different species of moth at heights ranging from 6,184ft (1,885m) to 12,057ft (3,675m) above sea level. Temperature measurements showed that the region had warmed by 0.7°C in 42 years. The findings of the survey, which echo studies in temperate zones where the upward shift has been detected, have serious implications for species diversity.

Many insects, larger animals and plants found on mountains are expected to move up the slopes in warmer conditions because temperatures generally fall as the altitude rises. As they reach higher elevations they rediscover their ideal temperature, but there is only so far they can go before running out of mountain. With many species found only in particular mountain ranges, sometimes confined to just a single peak, scientists fear that a large proportion will be driven into extinction as temperatures become too extreme for them to survive.

Scientists from the University of York in the United Kingdom led the expedition in collaboration with researchers from the National University of Tainan in Taiwan, the Malaysia Sabah University and the Forest Research Centre of Sabah in Malaysia, and the Natural History Museum in the UK.

opposite top:
Hand made trap
opposite below:
Mount Kinabalu
above left:
Moth in vegetation
above right:
Moth collection

Tree Deaths

Global warming has been named as the prime suspect as scientists attempt to discover why trees are dying more than twice as fast in parts of North America than they did half a century ago. Mortality rates have doubled in as few as seventeen years in some places, and researchers have warned that if it goes unchecked the make-up of forests could change dramatically.

Increases in the number of deaths were detected in established forests at least two hundred years old in the western US and the south-west of Canada. The problem was worst in the north-west where mortality rates doubled in seventeen years, but it was also identified in California where rates doubled in twenty-five years, and further inland where it took twenty-nine years. Increased death rates were found to be irrespective of the age of the trees, their size, their height, or the species, and the forests are losing them faster than they can be replaced.

Researchers reached their conclusions after taking measurements at 76 different forest locations and comparing them to data from monitoring that went back more than fifty years. Deaths had increased in 87 per cent of the test sites. After ruling out several possible causes the researchers cited warmer temperatures since 1955 as the most likely reason for the increase in the mortality rate. Temperatures rose by 0.3-0.5°C per decade from 1970 to 2006, and, though seemingly small, this rise was strong enough, scientists said, to reduce the amount of snow that accumulates in winter, to cause the snow to melt earlier in the year and to lengthen the summer drought.

The team of researchers, led by scientists at the US Geological Survey, suggested that the stress caused to the trees by the longer dry periods could be a contributory factor in speeding up death rates. They also said that higher temperatures could make it easier for pest insects and diseases to survive and spread. Warmer conditions have already been blamed for some outbreaks of bark beetle, which have killed many trees.

Warmer temperatures have been blamed for outbreaks of bark beetle which have killed many trees

Changes in tree mortality rates over a single year are small but when compounded over decades the effects have the potential to cause severe damage to the forests. Eventually the structure of the forests could change with much more thinly spread trees that are both younger on average and smaller. This would have potentially serious consequences for the animals and other plants living there.

The 76 forest locations where mortality was measured were in California, Oregon, Washington, Idaho, Arizona, New Mexico and Colorado in the US, and in British Columbia in Canada. Plots ranged in size from 0.25 hectares to 15.75 hectares and contained 58,736 trees, of which 11,095 died during the study period (1955 to 2007). The average age of the forests was 450 years, though some were more than a thousand years old.

Fossilised Warning

Six petrified forests are providing a snapshot of how global warming can radically alter the make-up of tropical landscapes and cause rainforests to collapse. It is more than 300 million years since the forests were green and lush but their preservation as fossils shows the changes they went through. The six forests date from 303.9 million to 309 million years ago and span a period of rising temperatures that levelled out 306.5 million years ago. When the first of the six forests, the earliest known to be preserved, was alive, the earth had ice caps, but the climate had switched to greenhouse conditions by the time the sixth was growing.

Huge horsetails, ferns and vast club moss trees that reached 100ft (30m) or more dominated rainforests 309 million years ago. As temperatures rose, the lush rainforest vegetation disappeared because the huge plants were unable to cope with the stresses caused by the heat. The plants that came to dominate the hotter landscape were much wispier ferns. It is thought that the coastal forests died when earthquakes caused the ground to subside and the sea poured in over them.

Palaeontologists led by Dr Howard Falcon-Lang of the University of Bristol in the UK were able to view the forests in more than fifty coal mines deep under the surface of modern-day Illinois, Indiana and Kentucky in the US. Most of the vegetation had turned to coal, but once it had been dug out it was possible to see the fossilised traces of enough plants and leaf litter to provide a detailed picture of the forest ecosystem.

In the tunnels researchers were able to see above their heads thousands of the stumps and roots of the drowned forests and often entire trees, which had come crashing down to be preserved lying on the ground. One of the forests covered 39 sq.miles (100sq.km) and is the biggest fossil forest yet discovered.

According to Dr Falcon-Lang the changes observed in the ancient vegetation as extreme global warming set in were suggestive of what will eventually happen to the modern-day Amazon rainforest if man-made climate change cannot be controlled. Members of the research team, which includes scientists from the Illinois State Geological Survey and the Smithsonian Institution in the US, hope that with further study they will be able to determine what caused the climate to change so dramatically more than 300 million years ago.

Catastrophe for Corals

A fifth of the world's corals have vanished in the last half century and the destruction is expected to intensify as the effects of climate change are felt. More than a quarter of reef-building corals are threatened with extinction and the figure is likely to rise significantly if global warming is not brought under control. Corals are sensitive to warmer and more acidic conditions, both of which are caused by the rise in carbon dioxide emissions that are widely accepted by scientists as driving global warming. In the atmosphere, carbon dioxide traps heat, warming the planet. In the oceans, it is absorbed by the water and makes the seas more acidic.

Of the 845 known species of reef-building corals, 27 per cent have been classified by the International Union for the Conservation of Nature (IUCN) as threatened, with a further 20 per cent close to being under threat. A decade ago only two per cent were considered to be endangered. A study conducted for the IUCN looked at 799 warm-water varieties and concluded that 566 of them are likely to be adversely affected by climate change. The impact on corals has damaging knock-on effects because so many other marine creatures rely on them for food and shelter – they are home to 25 per cent of marine species. In the worst cases entire ecosystems can be destroyed when corals die.

The corals of the Indo-Malay-Philippine Archipelago have the highest number of threatened species. Corals have also been badly affected in the Caribbean where two of the most important species, Staghorn Coral, *Acropora cervicornis*; and Elkhorn Coral, *Acropora palmate*; are now critically endangered.

Damage to corals is caused by a variety of factors but it is increasingly recognised that climate change is the single biggest threat. Research led by Dr Ken Anthony of the ARC Centre for Excellence for Coral Reef Studies concluded that the threat to corals was higher than previously thought because of increased acidity. Bleaching; the process by which symbiotic algae die or desert a coral; was previously thought to be caused primarily by increases in temperature, but the study found that acidity played a much more important role, raising fears that predictions of future bleaching had been underestimated. In particular, it was found that coralline algae, which hold reefs together and help coral larvae settle successfully, are highly sensitive to increased acidity, and their loss would severely damage the ability of reefs to grow. This was backed up by the work of scientists at the Carnegie Institution in the US and the Hebrew University of Jerusalem in Israel, which suggested that there was a serious threat that reefs would start dissolving and thus vanish all together.

The increased intensity and number of storms associated with climate change are further factors that have been found to be a threat to coral reefs. A study by Dr Jennie Mallela of the ARC Centre for Excellence for Coral Reef Studies and Professor James Crabbe of the University of Bedfordshire found that the storms and bleaching events disrupt the ability of the corals to grow. By looking at the history of corals around Tobago in the Caribbean since the 1980s they found that fresh growth in young corals dropped by as much as three quarters and fewer new colonies formed.

overleaf: **Staghorn coral with polyps open at night**

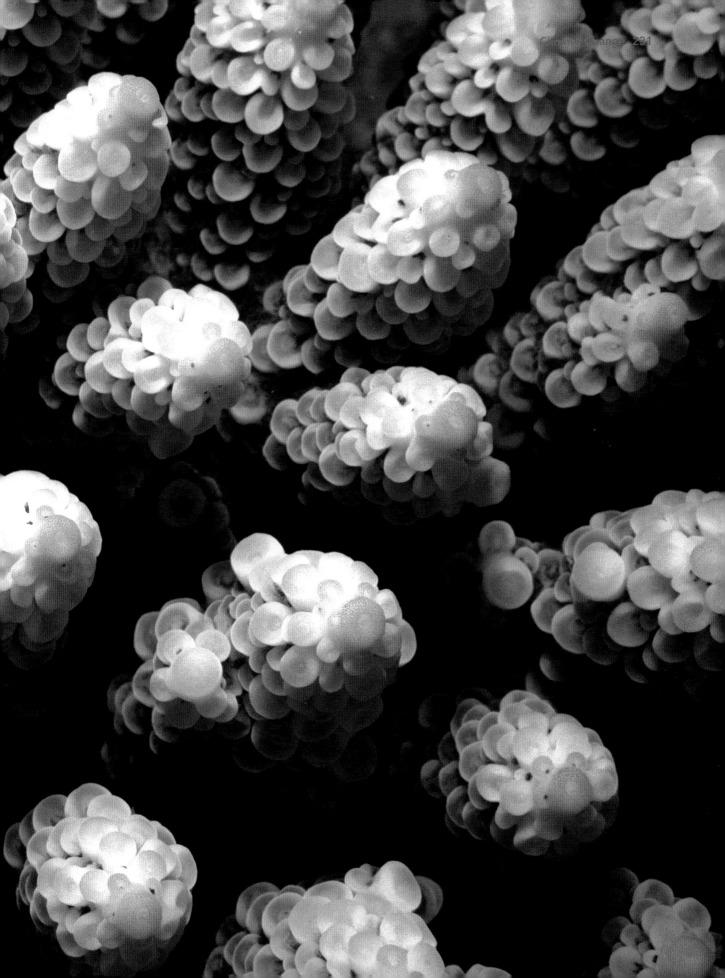

If You Can't Stand the Heat

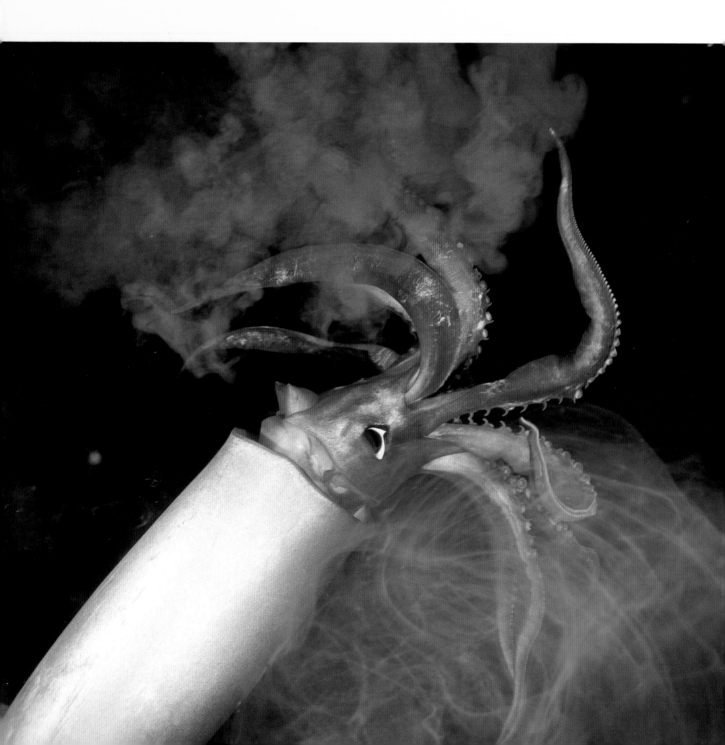

A voracious marine predator is likely to find it harder to catch its dinner by the end of the century because global warming will make it lethargic and slow-witted. Jumbo squid are among the fastest moving marine creatures when they rise to the oxygen-rich surface waters in schools of up to 1,200 individuals to feed in a jet-propelled frenzy. To maintain their furious pace of almost 15mph (24kph) they consume oxygen at a greater rate than almost any other animal in the sea.

However, one of the predicted effects of climate change is an increase in carbon dioxide levels in the upper layer of the oceans, resulting in lower oxygen levels. Researchers predict that any reduction in the availability of oxygen will have a calamitous effect on the squid. Swimming at slower speeds, the squid will be less able to catch its prey, which includes lanternfish, sardines and mackerel. Moreover, it will be far more difficult for it to escape predators such as the sperm whale.

Jumbo squid, *Dosidicus gigas*, also known as Humboldt squid, come up to surface waters at night to feed, but during daylight hours they swim at much lower depths. To survive the low oxygen levels at depths below 575ft (175m) the animals become much less active and reduce their metabolisms by 80 per cent.

To assess the likely effect on the squid, researchers from the University of Rhode Island in the US captured 86 of them from the Eastern Tropical Pacific. The squid were placed in chambers with conditions designed to mimic those forecast by climate models for 2100. It was found that in the higher carbon dioxide conditions, the squid reduced their metabolisms by 30 per cent and their activity levels by almost half. Part of the reason for returning to the shallower and better-oxygenated waters at night, aside from catching food, is that the squid need to recover from spending several hours in hypoxic conditions. If, as a result of climate change, the upper levels of the water fail to provide the high levels of oxygen the squid need to recover and feed, they will either have to become less active or move to new regions.

In the Eastern Pacific today, the squid, which can reach more than 6.5ft (2m) in length and weigh more than 110lbs (50kg), are already operating at the boundaries of their capabilities. Researchers describe them as forever living "on the edge of oxygen limitation" because all the oxygen taken into the body is used up within a single cycle of the blood around the body. According to Dr Rui Rosa, now of Lisbon University in Portugal, the ten-armed squid is likely to be forced closer and closer to the surface to find waters rich enough in oxygen to suit it, thus severely reducing the depth of water in which it can hunt effectively.

The anticipated rise in the temperature of the sea – by up to 3°C in the Eastern Tropical Pacific, according to the United Nations' Intergovernmental Panel on Climate Change – is in itself predicted to be a problem for the jumbo squid. It is already sensitive to warmth and can only put up with it for a few minutes before heading back into the depths to cool down. Higher temperatures prompted by climate change will only exacerbate this difficulty.

With future oxygen levels and temperatures both likely to prove a problem it is thought that the squid may attempt to find new hunting grounds. Such a movement will have a knock-on effect on the marine ecosystems around it, because, as a predator, it helps keep the numbers of prey species in check. Its disappearance would allow them to expand and upset the natural balance. Similarly, the large animals that prey on the squid would either have to follow it or take a bigger toll of other species in the region.

Ironically, a slight increase in sea temperature may be one of the factors contributing to the northward expansion of the jumbo squid's range, away from its traditional tropical and sub-tropical territories. It is now found as far north as Alaska. Scientists believe that overfishing of the species that eat squid, such as blue marlin, swordfish and sharks, could be another contributing factor.

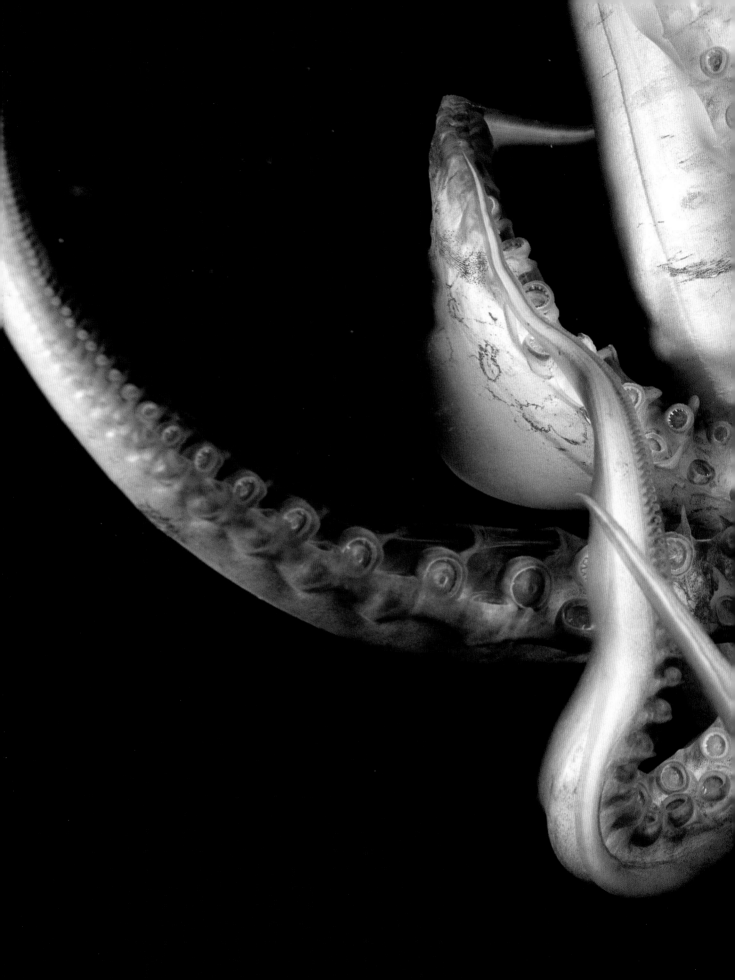

Index

Picture Credits

FRONT COVER:
Suzi Eszterhas / naturepl.com

BACK COVER,
pp. 1, 2, 128, 130, 132, 156: Alex Bernasconi

PRELIMINARIES
p. 3 © Chantal Steyn; p. 5 © Todd Marshall

INVASIVES
p. 10 © Mike Bailey and Steve Williams; p. 11 © Kate Kiefer; pp. 12-13 © Dr Tracy Langkilde, Pennsylvania State University; p. 14, top left © Prof Peter G Ryan; p. 14, top right © Hrafn Óskarsson; p. 14, bottom © Chantal Steyn; pp. 16-19 © Forest & Kim Starr; p. 20 © Isaac Chellman; p. 21, left © Haldre Rogers; p. 21, right © Ken Lucas / Getty; p. 22 © Mike Read/ naturepl.com; pp. 23-25 © Michael Dvorak / FCD / Darwin Initiative; pp. 26-27 © Dr Roger S Key; p. 28 © Bill Wakefield; p. 29 © Peter Birch

ANCIENTS
pp. 32-33 © Mauricio Anton; p. 34 © Mary L Droser; p. 35, top © Simon Powell, University of Bristol; p. 35, bottom © Markus Poschmann; pp. 36-39 © Tor Sponga, reproduced with permission from Oslo Natural History Museum, Norway; p. 40 © Luci Betti Nash; p. 41 © Zhao Chuang and Xing Lida; pp. 42, 44 © Dr Mark Witton. Originally published in Witton, M. P. & Naish, D. 2008. *A reappraisal of azhdarchid pterosaur functional morphology and paleoecology.* PLoS ONE 3(5): e2271 doi:10.1371/journal.pone.0002271; p. 46 © Ray Carson, University of Florida News Bureau; p. 47 © Jason Bourque, Florida Museum of Natural History; p. 48 © Dr John Long, Museum Victoria; p. 50 © Prof Derek Siveter. Originally published in Hou, Xianguang, Siveter, Derek J, Aldridge, Richard J. & Siveter, David J. 2008. *Collective behaviour in an Early Cambrian arthropod.* Science, 322, 224; p. 52, top © Fred Clouter; p. 52, bottom © Ludger Bollen, "*Der Flug des Archaeopteryx*", Quelle & Meyer Verlag; p. 54 © Martin Lipman, reproduced with permission from the Canadian Museum of Nature, Ottawa, Canada; pp. 56-57 © Todd Marshall; pp. 58-59 © Zhang Fucheng; p. 60

© Allison C. Daley, reproduced with permission from the Smithsonian National Museum of Natural History; pp. 62-63 © Dr Nick Longrich, University of Calgary; p. 66 © Megan Lorenz

EXTINCTION THREATS
p. 70, top left © Eleanor Briccetti; p. 70, top right © Meade Krosby; p. 70, bottom © Doug Greenberg; p. 72 © Bryn Jones; p. 74, 96, 150, 216 © Mark Carwardine / naturepl.com; p. 76 © Peter Oxford / naturepl.com; p. 78 © A. E. & R. Holt-White; p. 79 © Alastair Reid; pp. 80-81 © Dr Santiago Espinosa, with the support of WCS, WWF and University of Florida

CONSERVATION
p. 84 © Peter Reese / naturepl.com; p. 86 © Doug Perrine / naturepl.com; p. 89 © William Oliver / Durrell Wildlife Conservation Trust; pp. 90-91 © E. Bowen-Jones / Flora & Fauna International; p. 92 © Jennifer Goddard; p. 93 © Hugo Darras; p. 95 © Anup Shah / naturepl.com; p. 98 © Jean-Pierre Zwaenepoel / naturepl.com; p. 100 © Gerardo Garcia / Durrell Wildlife Conservation Trust; p. 102 © Landsat Image Mosaic of Antarctica (LIMA) Project; p. 103, top © British Antarctic Survey; p. 103, bottom © Chris Gilbert / British Antarctic Survey; p. 104 © Landsat Image Mosaic of Antarctica (LIMA) Project; pp. 106-107 © Eric Wakker; p. 108 © Reinhard / ARCO / naturepl.com; p. 110 © Dan Burton / naturepl.com; p. 112 © Peter Barham & Tilo Burghardt

REDISCOVERED SPECIES
p. 116 © Hanne & Jens Eriksen / naturepl.com; p. 119 © Hadoram Shirihai. Originally published in Shirihai, H. & Bretagnolle, V. In prep. *Albatrosses, petrels and shearwaters of the world: a handbook to their taxonomy, identification, ecology and conservation.* Christopher Helm, London; p. 120 © Guy Eisner; p. 123 © D Martyr / KSNP / Flora & Fauna International; p. 124 © RGB Kew; p. 125 © Colin Clubbe / RBG Kew

BEHAVIOUR
pp. 134-135 © Dr Udo Schmidt; p. 136 © Doug Perrine / naturepl.com; p. 138 © Nicholas

Mathevon; pp. 139-140 © Amelie Vergne; p. 142 © Wolfgang Stuppy; p. 143 © Dr Heather Whitney, University of Bristol & Dr. Beverley Glover, University of Cambridge; p. 144 © Paul Stinsa; pp. 146-147 © Richard Naylor, University of Sheffield; pp. 148-149 © Christian Nunes; p. 152 © Marco Gherlenda; p. 153 © Francesca Barbero; p. 154 © Alex Bernasconi; p. 155, left © Richard Byrne, University of St Andrews; p. 155, right © Katie Slocombe, University of St Andrews; p. 158 © John E Marriott / Getty; p. 159 © Prof Marco Musiani; p. 161 © Trond Larsen; pp. 162, 164 © Bill Love; p. 166 © Wolfgang Stuppy; p. 168 © Eric Baccega / naturepl.com; p. 169 © Dr Bryan Fry; p. 170 © Peter Scoones / naturepl.com; p. 174 © Timothy Morton; p. 176 © Bruce Davidson / naturepl.com

NEW SPECIES
p. 181 © John Sear; p. 182 © John Dransfield / RBG Kew; p. 183 © Nathalie Metz / RBG Kew; p. 184, top and bottom left © Nathalie Metz / RBG Kew; p. 184, right © John Dransfield/ RBG Kew; p. 186 © Richard Ling; p. 187 © Alessandro Catenazzi; p. 188 © Somsak Panha; p. 190 © Brandon Cole / naturepl.com; p. 192 © Sue Daly / naturepl.com; p. 194 © Lou Jost; p. 197 © Wayne Maddison, Beaty Biodiversity Museum, University of British Columbia; pp. 198-200 © Jeremy Holden / Flora & Fauna International; p. 202 © David Hall; p. 204 © Francesco Rovero; pp. 206-208 © Julian Bayliss / RBG Kew; p. 210 © Dr David Bowden / NIWA

CLIMATE CHANGE
p. 214 © Roy Mangersnes / naturepl.com; p. 218 © Jack Reynolds; p. 220 © Allan Howell; pp. 222-223 © Sandra Bouwhuis; p. 224, top © I-Ching Chen, University of York; p. 224, bottom © Kee Seng Chew; p. 225 © I-Ching Chen, University of York; p. 227 © Howard Falcon-Lang, Royal Holloway; p. 228 © Roberto Rinaldi / naturepl.co; p. 230 © Jeff Rotman / naturepl.com; pp. 232, 234 © Brian J. Skerry / Getty

Every effort has been made to contact and accurately credit all copyright holders, and we are grateful to the individuals and institutions who have assisted in this task. Where we have not succeeded, we apologise and welcome corrections for reprints and future editions.

Acknowledgments

A book, though usually attributed to a single author, is almost always the culmination of the efforts of many people and this one is no exception. I should like here to put on record my gratitude for all the help and encouragement I have received.

I must, in particular, thank my late publisher, Andreas Papadakis, without whom this book would never have been written. It was he who first proposed it and encouraged me to go ahead with it. Sadly, he died in 2008 before he could see his idea come to fruition. His daughter, Alexandra, carried on where he left off and despite all the calls on her time has been a source of great help and friendly encouragement. She has been involved from inception to completion and I owe especial thanks to her for the design of the pages. Others at Papadakis to whom I am indebted include Sarah Roberts who has worked tirelessly to track down pictures and to help edit and check the text. Similarly, I am grateful to Peter Liddle and Naomi Doerge for their picture research while Sheila de Vallée's editing and proof reading has been invaluable.

In writing about wildlife discoveries past and present I am entirely dependent on the work of thousands of scientists around the world who devote their lives to the pursuit, dissemination and application of knowledge. There are far too many to name individually but I am grateful and a little in awe of all of them. Many have also very kindly provided images.

Most of the discoveries described in this book were first reported in scientific journals which have been an invaluable source of information. Publications include *Acta Palaeontologica Polonica, Aqua – International Journal of Ichthyology, Biological Invasions, Biology Letters, BioScience, Bird Conservation International, BMC Ecology, Botanical Journal of the Linnean Society, Bulletin of the British Ornithologists' Club, Copeia, Cretaceous Research, Current Biology, Deep-Sea Research, Geological Magazine, Global Ecology and Biogeography, Journal of Applied Ecology, Molecular Ecology, Nature, PLoS ONE, Proceedings of the California Academy of Sciences, Proceedings of the National Academy of Sciences, Proceedings of the Royal Society B: Biological Sciences, Science, Zoological Journal of the Linnean Society* and *Zootaxa.* Other information has come from conversations with the scientists and their colleagues.

Finally, I should like to thank my family without whom far more than just this book would be impossible. In particular, my daughter Willow, whose enthusiasm is an infectious delight, and my wife, Heather Chinn, who has helped write, edit and organise and has been vital in so many other ways.